More Songs of the Seventies
The Decade Series

Contents

- 4   Afternoon Delight
- 12 All By Myself
- 9   All Right Now
- 14 American Pie
- 24 And I Love You So
- 30 Baby Come Back
- 36 Baby What A Big Surprise
- 27 Bennie And The Jets
- 40 Best Thing That Ever Happened To Me
- 44 Billy, Don't Be A Hero
- 48 The Boys Are Back In Town
- 52 Change Of Heart
- 60 Copacabana (At The Copa)
- 56 Could It Be Magic
- 67 Deja Vu
- 70 Different Worlds
- 74 Don't Give Up On Us
- 80 Don't Stop
- 86 Feelin' Stronger Every Day
- 90 Happy Days
- 83 Here Comes That Rainy Day Feeling Again
- 94 Honesty
- 102 Honky Cat
- 108 Hopelessly Devoted To You
- 99 Hurting Each Other
- 112 I Am...I Said
- 118 I Shot The Sheriff
- 120 I Write The Songs
- 124 I'm Not Lisa
- 127 If You Leave Me Now
- 132 Island Girl
- 136 It's Impossible (Somos Novios)
- 140 The Last Time I Felt Like This
- 143 Maggie May
- 146 Maybe I'm Amazed
- 149 Me And You And A Dog Named Boo
- 152 Neither One Of Us (Wants To Be The First To Say Goodbye)
- 158 Night Fever
- 163 One Tin Soldier
- 166 One Toke Over The Line
- 170 Pieces Of April
- 173 Please Come To Boston
- 176 Precious And Few
- 180 Ready To Take A Chance Again (Love Theme)
- 185 Right Time Of The Night
- 188 The Rockford Files
- 190 Sad Eyes
- 194 She Believes In Me
- 202 She's Always A Woman
- 200 Speak Softly, Love (Love Theme)
- 212 Where Do I Begin (Love Theme)
- 216 Wishing You Were Here
- 207 Year Of The Cat
- 220 You Make Lovin' Fun

T4-ABL-006

AFTERNOON DELIGHT

Words and Music by
BILL DANOFF

In a moderately slow country 2

Gon-na find my ba-by, gon-na hold her tight, gon-na grab some af-ter-noon de-light. My mot-to's al-ways been "When it's right, it's right," why wait un-til the mid-dle of a cold, dark night

Copyright © 1976 Cherry Lane Music Publishing Company, Inc.
International Copyright Secured   All Rights Reserved

PIANO • VOCAL • GUITAR

More Songs of the Seventies

THE DECADE SERIES

HAL•LEONARD CORPORATION
7777 W. BLUEMOUND RD. P.O. BOX 13819 MILWAUKEE, WI 53213

Copyright © 1994 by HAL LEONARD CORPORATION
International Copyright Secured   All Rights Reserved

For all works contained herein:
Unauthorized copying, arranging, adapting, recording or public performance is an infringement of copyright.
Infringers are liable under the law.

This publication is not for sale in the EC and/or Australia or New Zealand.

When ev-'ry-thing's a lit-tle clear-er in the light of day, And we know the night is al-ways gon-na be here an-y-way?

(1.,3.) Think-ing of you's work-ing up my ap-pe-tite, look-ing for-ward to a lit-tle af-ter-noon de-light. Rub-bing
(2.) out this morn-ing feel-ing so po-lite, I al-ways thought a fish could not be caught who did-n't bite. But you

sticks and stones to-geth-er make the sparks ig-nite And the thought of rub-bing you is get-ting
got some bait a-wait-ing and I think I might Like nib-bl-ing a lit-tle af-ter-

so ex-cit-ing. Sky rock-ets in flight,
noon de-light.

Af-ter-noon de-light,

af - ter-noon de-light,

Gm7 Am B♭ C7 F
3 fr
af - ter - noon de - light.
To Coda
1
2
Start - ed
Gm7 C7
3 fr
Be wait-ing for me, ba-by, when I come a - round.
Gm7 C7
3 fr
D.S. al Coda
We can make a lot of lov-ing 'fore the sun gone down.

CODA
Gm
3fr
Am
B♭
af -
C
F
af - ter - noon de - light,
no chord
af -
F
af - ter - noon de - light.

ALL RIGHT NOW

Words and Music by PAUL RODGERS
and ANDY FRASER

Moderately, with a strong beat

There she stood in the
I took her home to my

street
place

smil-ing from her head to her feet. I said,
watch-ing ev-'ry move on her face. She said,

"Hey, what is this?" Now ba-by, may-be may-be she's in need of a
"Look, what's your game ba-by, are you tryin' to put me in

Copyright © 1970, 1971 Blue Mountain Music Ltd.
All Rights for the U.S. and Canada Administered by Songs Of PolyGram International, Inc.
International Copyright Secured   All Rights Reserved

kiss.   I said, "Hey,   what's your   name ba-by,
shame?"   I said, "Slow,   don't go so fast,
may-be we can see things the same.   Now don't you wait ___ or
don't you think that love ___ can last?"   She said, ___ "Love,   Lord a-
hes-i-tate, ___   let's move ___ be-fore they raise the park-ing
bove, ___   now ___ you're tryin' to trick me in
rate."}
love."}   All   right   now ___ ba-by, it's all ___

right now. All right now baby, it's all right now.

All right now baby, it's all right now.

Repeat and Fade

ALL BY MYSELF

Words and Music by ERIC CARMEN
and SERGEI RACHMANINOFF

all by my self any-more. All by my self, don't wan-na live
all by my self any-more. Hard to be sure, some-times I
When I was young, I nev-er
feel so in-se-cure, and love so dis-tant and ob-scure
need-ed an-y-one, and ma-kin' love was just for fun;
re-mains the cure.
those days are gone.

D.S. and Fade

AMERICAN PIE

Words and Music by
DON McLEAN

Freely

A long, long time a-go I can still re-mem-ber how that mu-sic used to make me smile. And I knew if I had my chance that I could make those peo-ple dance and may-be they'd be hap-py for a while.

© Copyright 1971, 1972 by MUSIC CORPORATION OF AMERICA, INC. and BENNY BIRD MUSIC
Sole Selling Agent MCA MUSIC PUBLISHING, A Division of MCA INC., 1755 Broadway, New York, NY 10019
International Copyright Secured   All Rights Reserved
MCA music publishing

But Feb-ru-ar-y made me shiv-er with ev-'ry pa-per I'd de-liv-er.

Bad news on the door-step I could-n't take one more step I

can't re-mem-ber if I cried when I read a-bout his wid-owed bride,

Some-thing touched me deep in-side the day the mu-sic died.

So bye-bye, Miss American Pie. Drove my Chevy to the levee but the levee was dry. Them good ole boys were drinkin' whiskey and rye, Singin' this'll be the day that I die,

This - 'll be the day that I die.

1. Did you write the book of love and do you
2.-4. *See additional lyrics*

have faith in God a - bove? If the Bi - ble tells

you so Now do you be - lieve in

rock and roll. Can music save your mortal soul and can you teach me how to dance real slow? Well, I know that you're in love with him 'cause I saw you dancin' in the gym. You both kicked off your shoes.

Man, I dig those rhythm and blues. I was a lonely teenage broncin' buck with a pink carnation and a pick-up truck. But I knew I was out of luck the day the music died.

20

I start-ed sing-ing He was sing-in' bye - bye, Miss A-mer-i-can Pie__ Drove my Chev-y to the lev-ee but the lev-ee was dry.__ Them good ole boys__ were drink-in' whis-key and rye __ Sing-in' this-'ll be the day__ that I __ die, This-'ll be the day__ that I __

die.

rit.

Freely

I met a girl who sang the blues and I asked her for some hap-py news, But

she just smiled and turned a-way.

I went down to the sa-cred store where I heard the mu-sic years be-fore But the man there said the music would-n't play. And in the streets the chil-dren screamed, the lov-ers cried and the po-ets dreamed. But not a word was spo-ken the church bells all were bro-ken. And the three men I ad-mire most, the Fa-ther, Son and the Ho-ly Ghost, They caught the last train for the coast the

Additional Lyrics

2. Now for ten years we've been on our own,
   And moss grows fat on a rollin' stone
   But that's not how it used to be
   When the jester sang for the king and queen
   In a coat he borrowed from James Dean
   And a voice that came from you and me
   Oh and while the king was looking down,
   The jester stole his thorny crown
   The courtroom was adjourned,
   No verdict was returned
   And while Lenin read a book on Marx
   The quartet practiced in the park
   And we sang dirges in the dark
   The day the music died
   We were singin'... bye-bye... etc.

3. Helter-skelter in the summer swelter
   The birds flew off with a fallout shelter
   Eight miles high and fallin' fast,
   it landed foul on the grass
   The players tried for a forward pass,
   With the jester on the sidelines in a cast
   Now the half-time air was sweet perfume
   While the sergeants played a marching tune
   We all got up to dance
   But we never got the chance
   'Cause the players tried to take the field,
   The marching band refused to yield
   Do you recall what was revealed
   The day the music died
   We started singin'... bye-bye... etc.

4. And there we were all in one place,
   A generation lost in space
   With no time left to start again
   So come on, Jack be nimble, Jack be quick,
   Jack Flash sat on a candlestick
   'Cause fire is the devil's only friend
   And as I watched him on the stage
   My hands were clenched in fists of rage
   No angel born in hell
   Could break that Satan's spell
   And as the flames climbed high into the night
   To light the sacrificial rite
   I saw Satan laughing with delight
   The day the music died
   He was singin'... bye-bye... etc.

AND I LOVE YOU SO

Moderately slow

Words and Music by
DON McLEAN

1.,3. And I love you so,
2. And you love me too,

The peo-ple ask me how,
Your thoughts are just for me,

How I've lived till now,
You set my spir-it free,

I tell them I don't know.
I'm hap-py that you do.

I guess they un-der-stand,
The book of life is brief,

How lone-ly life has been,
And once a page is read,

© Copyright 1970, 1973 by MUSIC CORPORATION OF AMERICA, INC. and BENNY BIRD MUSIC
Sole Selling Agent MCA MUSIC PUBLISHING, A Division of MCA INC., 1755 Broadway, New York, NY 10019
International Copyright Secured   All Rights Reserved
MCA music publishing

But life be-gan a-gain, / All but love is dead, the day you took my / That is my be-lief. hand.

And, yes, I know how lonely life can be, (love-less) the night won't set me free. The shadows follow me and the But I don't let the

Dm7
eve - ning get me down,
(bring)
Now that you're a -
G7 G7♭9
1 C C6 C C6
2 C C6
round
me.
me.
C C6
D.S. al Coda
CODA
F G7
I tell them
I don't
C
know.
Dm C F Fm C
rit.

BENNIE AND THE JETS

Words and Music by ELTON JOHN
and BERNIE TAUPIN

Slow tempo

Hey kids, shake it loose to-geth-er the spot-
Hey kids, plug in-to the faith-less may-
3rd time piano solo
Ad lib. solo 3rd time

-light's hit-ting some-thing that's been known to change the wea-ther. We'll kill the fat-ted calf to-night, so stick a-round-
-be they're blinded but Ben-nie makes them age-less. We shall sur-vive, let us take our-selves a-

-long. You're gon-na hear e-lec-tric mus-ic sol-id walls of sound.
Where we fight our par-ents out in the streets to find who's right and who's wrong.

Copyright © 1973 Dick James Music Limited
All Rights for the United States and Canada Administered by Songs Of PolyGram International, Inc.
International Copyright Secured   All Rights Reserved

C
G
(3rd time vocal) Say Can-dy and Ron - nie have you seen them yet but
(no solo 3rd time)
Am
C
they're so spaced out Ben-nie and the Jets
G
Am
But they're weird and they're won-der-ful oh Ben - nie She's real-ly keen She's got e -
C
D
Em
Em7
lec-tric boots a mo-hair suit you know I read it in a mag - a - zine oh

C
Bb/C
D
Gmaj7
G6
Gmaj7
To Coda
Ben - nie and the Jets
Fmaj7
G7
1
Am/G
2
D.S. (Piano solo) al Coda
CODA
Ben - nie
Ben - nie
Repeat and Fade
Ben - nie Ben - nie Ben - nie Ben - nie and the Jets

BABY COME BACK

Words and Music by JOHN C. CROWLEY
and PETER BECKETT

Moderately Slow

Ab/Bb
Gm7
all my nights, all my mon - ey go-in' out on the town.
All day long wear-in' a mask of false bra-va-do,
Ab/Bb
Gm7
Do-in' an - y-thing just to get you off of my mind. But when the
try'n' to keep up a smile that hides a tear. But as the
Ab/Bb
Gm7
morn-ing comes, I'm right back where I start - ed a - gain. And
sun goes down, I get that emp-ty feel - ing a - gain.
Ab/Bb
Bb/C
C
try'n' to for-get you is just a waste of time.
How I wish to God that you were here.
Ba - by come back,

A♭maj7
Gm7
3fr
Cm
3fr
any kind of fool could see there was
Fm7
Gm7
3fr
Cm
3fr
something in ev'rything about you. Baby come back,
A♭maj7
Gm7
3fr
Cm
3fr
you can blame it all on me. I was
Fm7
Gm7
3fr
To Coda
1
Cm
3fr
D♭maj7
wrong and I just can't live without you.

you.

Now that I've pulled it all together, give me the chance to make you see.

G♭maj7
Fm7
B♭m
Have you used up all the love in your heart? _
B♭sus
8va
Noth - in' left for me, ain't there noth - in' left for me? _
no chord
loco
D.S. al Coda
_ Ba - by come back,
CODA
Cm
3fr
_ you. I was
dim.
mp
Fm7
Gm7
no chord
wrong _ and I just _ can't live... Ba - by come back,
mf

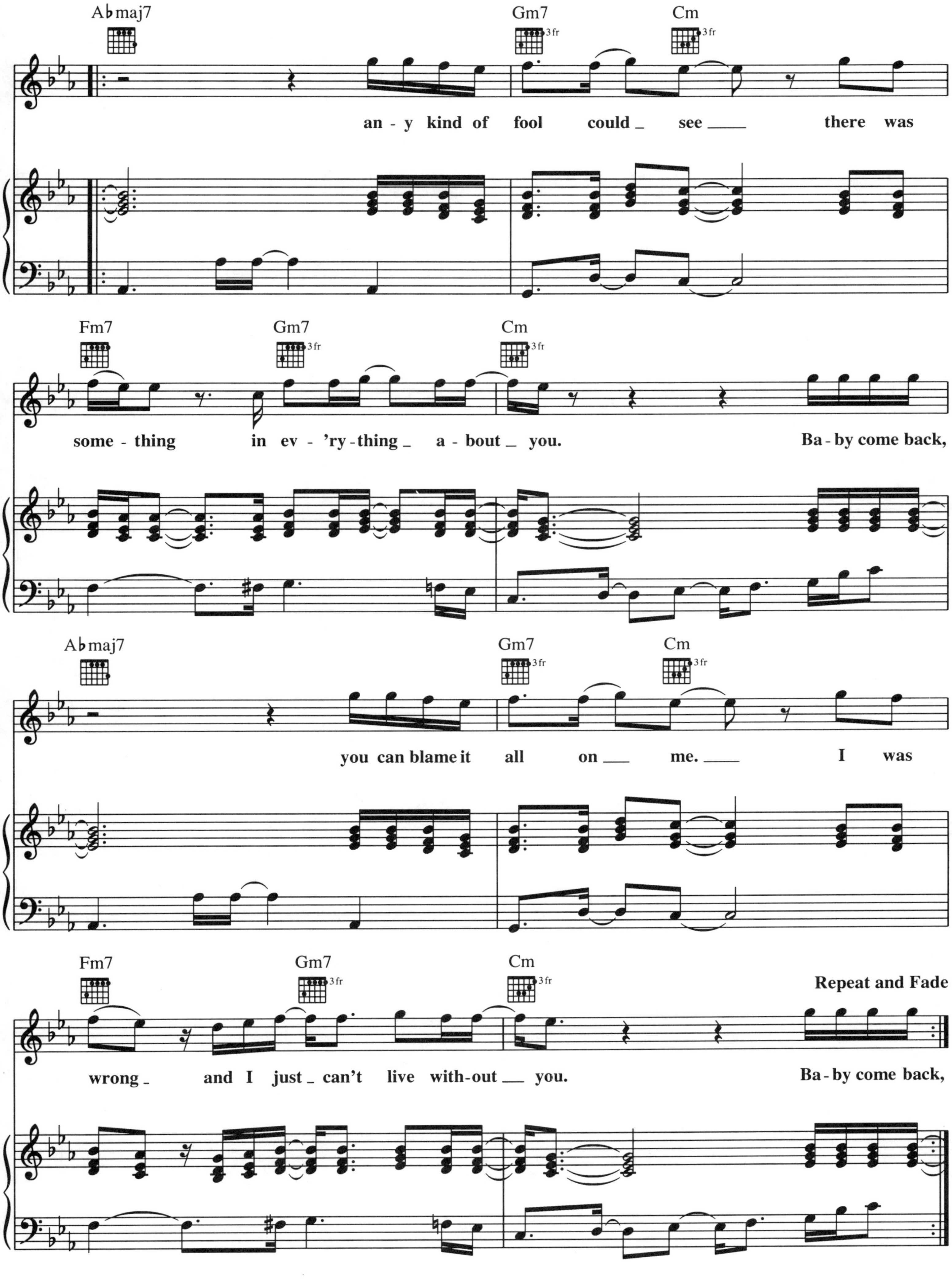

BABY WHAT A BIG SURPRISE

Words and Music by
PETER CETERA

Ba - by, what a big sur - prise; right be - fore my ver - y eyes, oh, oh, oh, oh. oh, oh, oh.

Just to be a - lone was a lit - tle more than I could take,

Am G C
then you came to stay. Oo.
Am G Am G/B C
Hold me in the morn - ing, love me in the af - ter - noon.
Am G B♭ G/B
Help me find my way, hey, yeah.
C Dm7 C7/E F C/E Dm
Now and then just like be - fore I think

C
Dm7
C7/E
Fsus
F
C/E
Dm
a - bout the love I've thrown a - way, but now
C
Dm7
C7/E
F
C7/E
it does - n't mat - ter an - y - way.
B♭
C
F
C/E
Dm7
Ba - by, what a big sur - prise;
B♭
C
F
E♭
3fr
B♭
Repeat and Fade
right be-fore my ve - ry eyes, oh, oh, oh, oh.

Best Thing That Ever Happened To Me

Words and Music by
JIM WEATHERLY

Moderately
no chord

mp legato

With pedal throughout

I've had my share of life's
have been times when the
ups and downs, but fate's been kind, the downs have been few.
times were hard, but always somehow I made it through.

Copyright © 1972 PolyGram International Publishing, Inc.
International Copyright Secured   All Rights Reserved

I guess you could say
But for ev-'ry that I've been luck-y, mo-ment I've spent hurt-ing, and I there was a guess you could say it's all be-cause of you. mo-ment spent lov-ing you.
If an-y-one should ev-er write my life

story _____ for what - ev - er

rea - son there might be, you'd be

there _____ be - tween each line _____ of pain and

glo - ry, _____ 'cause you're the best thing ____ that ev - er

43

BILLY, DON'T BE A HERO

Words and Music by PETER CALLENDER
and MITCH MURRAY

Reflectively

Gm **C7** **F**

1. The march-ing band came down a-long Main street, the sol-dier blues fell
2. The sol-dier blues were trapped on a hill side, the bat-tle rag-ing
3. I heard his fi-an-cée got a let-ter that told how Bil-ly

Gm **C7**

in be-hind. I looked a-cross and there I saw Bil-ly,
all a-round. The ser-geant cried, "We've got to hang on, boys,
died that day. The let-ter said that he was a he-ro,

F **Gm**

To Coda

wait-ing to go and join the line. And with her head up-
we've got to hold this piece of ground. I need a vol-un-
she should be proud he died that way.

Copyright © 1973 Dick James Music Ltd.
All Rights for the United States and Canada Administered by PolyGram International Publishing, Inc.
International Copyright Secured   All Rights Reserved

on his shoul - der, *his young and love - ly fi - an - cée,*
teer to ride___ up *and bring us back some ex - tra men."*

From where I stood___ I saw she was cry - ing, *and through her tears I*
And Bil - ly's hand___ was up in a mo - ment, *for - get - ting all the*

Chorus:
heard her say; *She said,* ⎫
words she said. ⎭ *"Bil - ly, don't be a he - ro, don't be a*

fool with your life.___ *Bil - ly, don't be a*

hero, come back and make me your wife." And as they start-ed to go she said, "Bil-ly, keep your head low. Bil-ly, don't be a he-ro, come back to me.'

I heard she threw that letter a-way.

Repeat and Fade

THE BOYS ARE BACK IN TOWN

Words and Music by
PHILIP PARRIS LYNOTT

Moderately bright, with a steady 4 beat

Verse

1. Guess who just got back to-day? Them wild-eyed boys that had been a-way. Had-n't changed, had-n't much to say, But, man, I still think them cats are cra-zy. They were ask-ing if you
2., D.S. (See additional verses)

Copyright © 1976 by Pippin-The-Friendly-Ranger Music Co. Ltd. (PRS)
All Rights Administered by Chappell & Co. (ASCAP)
International Copyright Secured   All Rights Reserved

Bm
C
Eb
were a - round,
How you was, where you could be found.
Bm
Em
Am
I told them you were liv - ing down - town,
Driv - ing all the old men
Am/D
G(no3rd)
Chorus
cra - zy.
The boys are back in town, the boys are back in town.
A(no3rd)
C(no 3rd)
G(no3rd)
I say, the boys are back in town,
the

(Fade after 3rd Chorus)

Additional Verses:

2. You know that chick that used to dance a lot
   Every night she'd be on the floor shaking what she'd got
   Man, when I tell you she was cool, she was hot
   I mean she was steaming.

   And that time over at Johnny's place
   Well, this chick got up and she slapped Johnny's face
   Man, we just fell about the place
   If that chick don't wanna know, forget her.

   (Chorus & Interlude)

3. Friday night they'll be dressed to kill
   Down at Dino's Bar and Grill
   The drink will flow and blood will spill
   And if the boys want to fight, you better let 'em

   That jukebox in the corner blasting out my favorite song
   The nights are getting warmer, it won't be long
   It won't be long till summer comes
   Now that the boys are here again.

   (Chorus and Fade)

CHANGE OF HEART

Words and Music by
ERIC CARMEN

Moderately, with a beat

I can still re-call when we said that our love was for-ev-er.
find some-one more than will-ing to be your re-place-ment.

All those plans we made for to-mor-
But there's no one else who can move

Copyright © 1978 Eric Carmen Music, Inc.
All Rights Administered by Songs Of PolyGram International, Inc.
International Copyright Secured   All Rights Reserved

row that looked so bright. And I
me the way you do. So for
un-der-stand all the rea-sons you gave me for leav-
now, good-bye. But if ev-er you find you still want
ing.
me, But that does-n't help when I'm
you just call my name, 'cause I'll
sleep-ing a-lone each night.
al-ways be here for you.
So if you

ev-er have a change of heart, just re-mem-ber it's not too late to start if you still be-lieve in what love can do.

I could

Abmaj7
4 fr.
Bb/Ab
Gm7
3 fr.
Noth-ing you could ev-er do can change the things I know deep
Bb/C
C
Abmaj7
4 fr.
Bb/Ab
in my heart. So I've got to make you un-der-stand be-fore I go.
Gm7
3 fr.
Bb/C
C
Bb/C
C
Soon-er or lat - er, I don't know when, I'm gon-na
Am7
D
Am7
D
D. S. and fade
get you back in my arms a - gain. And if you

COULD IT BE MAGIC

Words and Music by
ADRIENNE ANDERSON and BARRY MANILOW

An - gel of __ my life __ time, an - swer to __ all an -
Build-ing my world a - round __ you, nev - er leave you till __

_ swers I can find; Ba - by I love __ you.
_ my life __ is done; Ba - by I love __ you.

Come, come, come in - to my __ arms.
Now, come, now, now and hold on __ fast.

Let me know __ the won - der of all __ of you. __
Could this be __ the mag - ic at last? __

To Coda ⊕
(after 1st ending)

Ba - by I want you.

tacet

D.S. al Coda 𝄋

CODA
G7 (F Bass)
Cm (Eb Bass)
G (D Bass)
Cm
Ab (C Bass)
Could it be mag- ic?
Come, come,
Now, now,
Gmaj9 (B Bass)
G (B Bass)
Bbmaj7
Bb6
Am7
come in- to my arms.
now and hold on fast.
Let me know the won-
Could this be the mag-
Ab7
Gsus4
G
1.2. G7 (FBass)
Cm (Eb Bass)
G (D Bass)
3. G
Cm
der of all of you
ic at last?
Ba- by I want you.
Could it be mag - ic?
Fm
G7
Cm
Ab
Db
G7+5
G7
Cm

COPACABANA
(AT THE COPA)

Words by BRUCE SUSSMAN and JACK FELDMAN
Music by BARRY MANILOW

Moderately, with a Latin 'feel'

Fm7   Bb11   Ebmaj7

1. Her name was Lo - la; she was a show - girl with yel - low
2. (His name was) Ri - co; he wore a dia - mond, He was es -
3. (Her name is) Lo - la; she was a show - girl, But that was

Am7-5   D7   Gm(maj 7)   Gm7   Gm6

feath - ers in her hair and a dress cut down to there. She would Mer -
cort - ed to his chair, he saw Lo - la danc - ing there. And when she
thir - ty years a - go when they used to have a show. Now it's a

Copyright © 1978 Careers-BMG Music Publishing, Inc., Appoggiatura Music, Inc. and Camp Songs Music
International Copyright Secured   All Rights Reserved

Fm7 Bb11 Ebmaj7 Am7-5 D7
en - gue__ and do the Cha - Cha,__ And while she tried to be a star, To - ny
fin - ished,__ he called her o - ver.__ But Ri - co went a bit too far, To - ny
Dis - co,___ but not for Lo - la.___ Still in the dress she used to wear, fad - ed
Gm7 Cdim Gm
al - ways tend - ed bar, a - cross the crowd - ed___ floor. They worked from
sailed a - cross the bar. And then the punch - es___ flew and chairs were
feath - ers in her hair, She sits there so re - fined and drinks her -
Cdim D7-9 Gm Cm7 D7
eight to___ four. They were young and they had each oth - er, who could
smashed in___ two. There was blood and a sin - gle gun - shot, but just
self half___ blind. She lost her youth and she lost her To - ny, now she's

Gm D7 (F♯ bass) B♭7 (F bass) Fm7 B♭11 E♭maj7
ask for more? / who shot who? / lost her mind! At the Co - pa, Co - pa - ca - ba - na, The
f
Fm7 B♭11 E♭maj7 C11 C7 Fm7 B♭11
hot - test spot north of Ha - va - na. At the Co - pa, Co - pa - ca
C11 C7 Fm7 B♭7 Gm7 C9
ba - na, mu - sic and pas - sion were al - ways the fash - ion, At the
Fm7 D7-9 Gm9 F♯m9
To Coda
Co - pa
they fell in love.
she lost her love.
Love,
mf

Fm9
F#m9 Gm9
F#m9
1.
Fm9 F#m9 Gm9
Co - pa - ca - ba - na.
2. His name was
2. Fm9
F#m9
Interlude:
Gm9
Ab m9 4 fr.
Am9 5fr
Co - pa,
Co - pa - ca -
poco a poco cresc.
Bb m9 6 fr.
Bm9 7 fr.
Cm9 8fr
Db m9 9fr
ba - na,
Co - pa - ca - ba - na,
f
Ah,

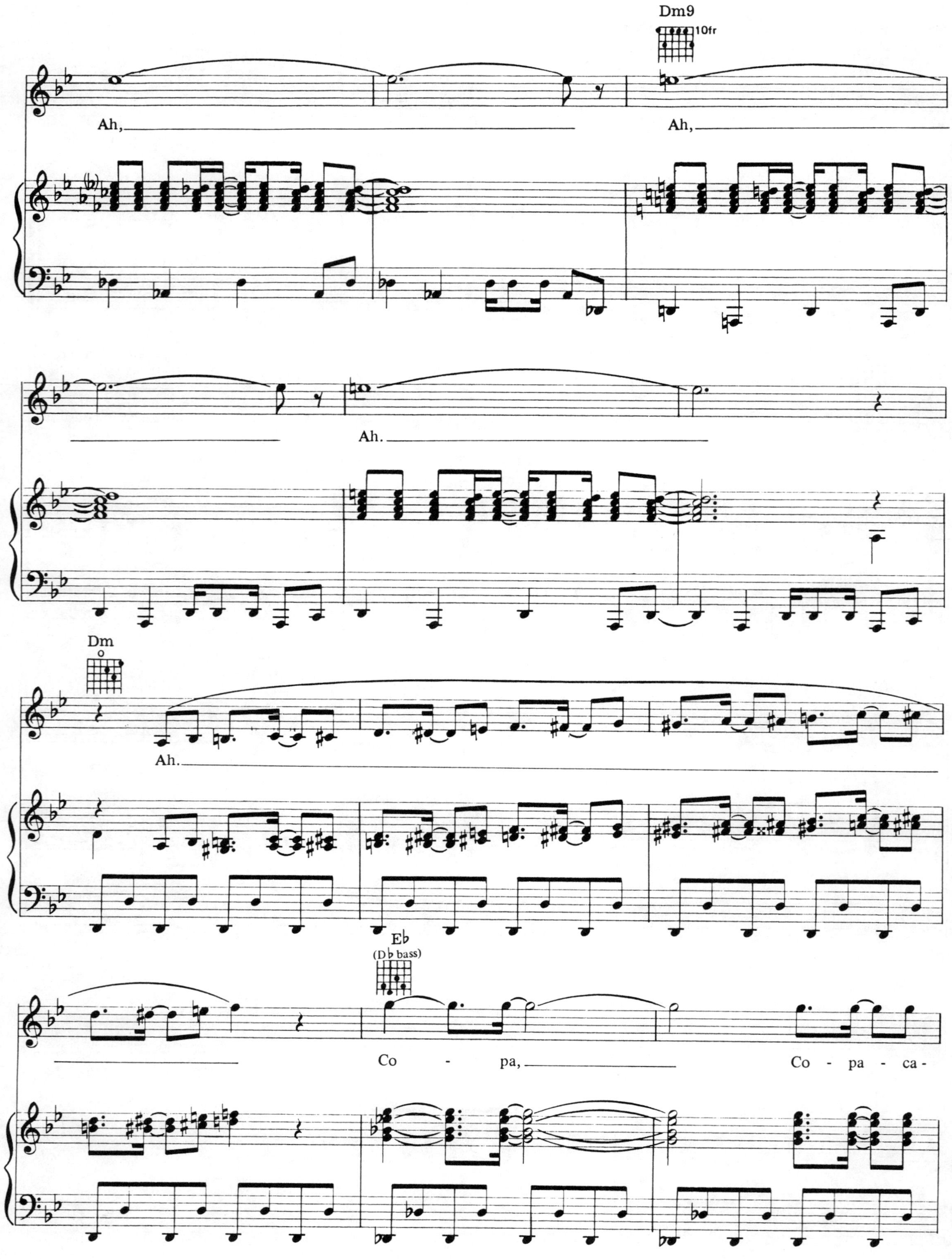
Dm9
10fr
Ah,
Ah,
Ah.
Dm
Ah.
E♭
(D♭ bass)
Co - pa,
Co - pa - ca -

ba - na,_____ like in__ Ha - va - na,

have a ba - na - na,_____ mu - sic__ and

pas - sion_____ al - ways__ in fash - ion.

Instrumental Solo

Fm9
F♯m9
Gm9
A♭m9
Am9
4 fr.
5fr
Gm9
F♯m9
Fm9
D. S. al Coda
Her name is
Coda
D7-9
Co - pa, —
don't fall in love,
Co - pa - ca -
don't fall in
ba - na, —
love.
Co - pa - ca - ba - na. —
mf
f

DEJA VU

Lyrics by ADRIENNE ANDERSON
Music by ISAAC HAYES

Moderately slow

like a love I used to know, long ago.
in a place I used to know, long ago.

De - ja - vu,

could you be the dream that I once knew? Is it you?
could you be the dream that I might come true, Shin - ing

De - ja - vu through? I keep re - mem - ber - ing me, I keep re -

Additional Verses:

Verse 3 This is divine; I've been waiting all my life, filling time.
Looking for you, nights were more than you could know, long ago.

Verse 4 Come to me now; we don't have to dream of love, we know how.
Somewhere before it's as if I loved you so long ago. *(To Chorus:)*

DIFFERENT WORLDS
(From The Paramount Television Series "ANGIE")

Words NORMAN GIMBEL
Music by CHARLES FOX

Moderately, with a strong beat

Let the time flow,_ let the love grow,_ let the rain_ show'r,_ let the rose_ flow'r._ Love, it seeks;_ and love, it finds;_ love, it con-quers; love,_ it binds. We come_ to each oth-er_ from

Copyright © 1979 by Bruin Music Company
International Copyright Secured   All Rights Reserved

dif-f'rent worlds;__ drawn to each oth-er _____ by the
love in-side_ of us.__ We give to each oth-er ___ our
dif-f'rent worlds._ Long as we __ can do it, _____
life, we're gon-na breeze_ right thru it._____ Let ___ the

time flow, let the love grow, let the rain show'r, let the rose flow'r. Love, it seeks; love, it finds; love, it con-quers; love, it binds; love, it seeks, and love, it finds.
Love, it con-quers; love, it binds; love, it seeks, and love, it

finds. _____
Oo, _____ oo, _____

Love, it con - quers; love, it binds; _____ love, it seeks, _____ and love, _____ it

finds. _____

DON'T GIVE UP ON US

Words and Music by
TONY MACAULAY

Moderately slow

1. Don't give up on us ba-by, ___ don't make the wrong seem more right,
(2., D.S.) up on us ba-by ___ we're still worth one more try, the fu-ture is-n't just one ___ night,
and tho' we put a last one ___ by, ___

Copyright © 1976 Macaulay Music Ltd.
All Rights for the U.S. and Canada Administered by PolyGram International Publishing, Inc.
International Copyright Secured   All Rights Reserved

D
A/C♯
To Coda
1
D
it's writ-ten in the moon - light
just for a rain - y eve - ning
and paint-ed on the stars,
A/C♯
Bm7
D/E
we can't change ours.
Don't give
2
D
C♯sus
C♯
Bm7
Dmaj7/A
when may-be stars are few.
Don't give up on us I know
D/E
A
A7
we can still come through
I

near-ly lost my head last night, __ you've got a right to stop be-liev-ing. __ There's still a lit-tle __ love left ev-en so.

Don't give up on us ba-by __ Lord knows we've

come this far, why can't we stay the way we __ are? __ The an-gel and the dream-er __ who some-times plays a fool. Don't give up on us I __ know we can still come through.

Instrumental solo

It's writ-ten in the moon-light _ and paint-ed on the stars, _ we can't change ours. Don't give

Solo ends

D.S. al Coda

CODA
D
C♯sus
4 fr
C♯
Bm7
2 fr
Dmaj7/A
when may-be stars are few. Don't give up on us I ___ know
D/E
A
Amaj7/G♯
we can still come through. ___ Don't give
Dmaj7/F♯
A/E
D
up on us ba - by, ___ don't give up on us ba - by. ___
D/E
A(add9)

DON'T STOP

Words and Music by
CHRISTINE McVIE

Moderate Rock shuffle

If you wake up and
Why not think a-bout
All I want is to

don't want to smile;___ if it takes just a
times ___ to come,___ and not a-bout just the ___
see you ___ smile, ___ if it takes just a

Copyright © 1976, 1977 by Fleetwood Mac Music
All Rights Administered by Careers-BMG Music Publishing, Inc.
International Copyright Secured All Rights Reserved

lit - tle while, / things that you've done. / lit - tle while.
o - pen your eyes and / If your life was / I know you don't be -

look at the day. / bad to you, / lieve that it's true.
You'll see things in a / just think what to - / I nev - er meant an - y

dif - f'rent way. / mor - row will do. / harm to you.
Don't stop

think - ing a - bout to - mor - row. Don't stop

A
E
D/E
It - 'll soon be here.
It - 'll be
A
B
bet - ter than be - fore.
Yes - ter - day's gone.
Yes -
1,2
3
- ter - day's gone.
- ter - day's gone.
E
D/E
Ooh,
A
E
D/E
A
Repeat and Fade
don't you look back.

HERE COMES THAT RAINY DAY FEELING AGAIN

Words and Music by TONY MACAULAY, ROGER COOK and ROGER GREENAWAY

1.-3. Here comes that rainy day feeling again
2. Here comes that rainy day feeling again

And soon love's tears will be falling like rain
And I'll be dreaming of you baby and then

It always seems to be a Monday   Left over mem-
Your face is always on my mind girl   I'm hoping soon

Copyright © 1970 Dick James Music Ltd.
All Rights for the United States and Canada Administered by PolyGram International Publishing, Inc.
International Copyright Secured   All Rights Reserved

C
Em
- o - ries of Sun - day al - ways spent with you Be - fore the clouds
you're gon - na find girl your way back to me 'Cause if you say
F
Dm
To Coda
1. G7
2. G7
ap - peared and took a - way my sun - shi - ine
you'll stay the
rain - y days will go a - way
C
B♭
Cm
Mis - ty morn - ing eyes I'm try - ing to dis - guise the way I feel

But I just can't hide it peo-ple seem to know the lon-li-ness must show I'm think-ing of my pride but break-ing up in-side girl_____

D.S. al Coda

CODA

took a-way the sun-shi-ine____ Here comes_ that rain-y day feel-ing a-gain__

Repeat and Fade

Here comes_ that rain-y day feel-ing a-gain__

FEELIN' STRONGER EVERY DAY

Words and Music by PETER CETERA
and JAMES PANKOW

Moderately slow

I do be-lieve in you and I know you be-lieve in me.
I know we real-ly tried to-geth-er, we had a love in-side.

Oh, yes; Oh, yes. But now we've re-al-ized
Oh, yes; Oh, yes. So, now the time has come for

love's not all that it's s'posed to be. Oh, yes;
both of us to live on the run. Oh, yes;

Copyright © 1973 by BMG Songs, Inc., Moose Music and Big Elk Music
International Copyright Secured   All Rights Reserved

Eb Bb F
Am7
Oh, yes.
Oh, yes.
And know - ing that you would have
Dm7
Am7
want - ed it this way,
I do be - lieve I'm feel - in'
Dm7
G
1
2
strong - er ev - 'ry day.
G C F
Dm7 Dm/F G
C F
Yeah, yeah, yeah.
Yeah, yeah, yeah;

88

I know that we both a - gree, the best thing to hap - pen to you, is the best thing that hap - pened to me.

Yeah, yeah, yeah. Feel - in' strong - er ev - 'ry day.

Repeat ad lib. and Fade

HAPPY DAYS
(Theme From The Paramount Television Series "HAPPY DAYS")

Words by NORMAN GIMBEL
Music by CHARLES FOX

Sun-day, Mon-day, hap-py days! Tues-day, Wednes-day, hap-py days! Thurs-day, Fri-day, hap-py days! Sat-ur-day, what a day. Rock-ing all week with you.

Copyright © 1974 by Bruin Music Company
International Copyright Secured   All Rights Reserved

F
Dm
This day is ours.
B♭
C
F
Won't you be mine?
This day is ours.
Dm
B♭
C
Oh, please be mine.
F
Hel - lo, sun - shine, good - bye rain. She's

wear-ing my school ring on a chain.

She's my stead-y, I'm her man.

I'm gon-na love her all I can. This day is ours.

Won't you be mine?

Lyrics:

This day is ours. _____ Oh, please be mine. _____

These hap - py days _____ are yours and mine. _____

These hap - py days _____ are yours and mine, _____ hap - py days!

HONESTY

Words and Music by
BILLY JOEL

Slowly

1. If you search for tenderness,
2. I can always find someone

it isn't hard to find. You can have the love you need to live.
to say they sympathize if I wear my heart out on my sleeve.

And if you look for truthfulness you might
But I don't want some pretty face to

© 1978 IMPULSIVE MUSIC
All Rights Controlled and Administered by EMI APRIL MUSIC INC.
All Rights Reserved   International Copyright Secured   Used by Permission

F
C bass
A
C♯bass
Dm
E♭
A7
just as well ___ be blind; ___ it al-ways seems to be ___ so hard ___ to give. ___
tell me pret-ty lies. ___ All I want ___ is some-one to be-lieve. ___
Dsus
D
E♭maj7
F7
D
F♯bass
Gm7
F
Hon - es-ty ___ is such a lone - ly word. ___
E♭
F
B♭
D
E♭maj7
F7
Ev-'ry-one is so un-true. ___ Hon - es-ty ___ is

hard-ly ev-er heard,_____ but most-ly what I need from you._____

I can find a lov-er, I can find a friend,_

I can have se-cur-i-ty un-til the bit-ter end.

An-y-one can com-fort me with prom-is-es a-gain. I know

I know.

When I'm deep in-side of me don't be too con-cerned.

I won't __ ask for noth-in' while I'm gone.

When I __ want sin-cer-i-ty, tell me, where __ else can I turn? __ Cause

you're the one __ that I __ de-pend up-on. __

HURTING EACH OTHER

Words by PETER UDELL
Music by GARY GELD

Moderately slow and steady

No one in the world ever had a love as sweet as my love, for no-where in the world could there be a boy as true as you love. All my

Clos-er than the leaves on a weep-in' wil-low, ba-by, we are. Clos-er, dear, are we than the sim-ple let-ters "A" and "B" are. All my

Copyright © 1965 PolyGram International Publishing, Inc. and Andrew Scott, Inc.
Copyright Renewed
International Copyright Secured   All Rights Reserved

Fm7
A♭/B♭
Cmaj9
love I give glad - ly to you, all your love you give
life I could love on - ly you, all your life you could
D/C
Fmaj7
C/E
Dm7
Dm7/G
glad - ly to me. Tell me why then, oh why should it be that
love on - ly me. Tell me why then, oh why should it be that
mf
C
Dm7/C
C
we go on hurt - ing each oth - er! We go on
f
Dm7/C
C
Dm7/C
C
hurt - ing each oth - er! Mak - ing each oth - er cry, hurt - ing each oth - er with

101

out ev-er know-ing why.

Can't we stop hurting each oth-er! Got-ta stop hurt-ing each oth-er! Mak-ing each oth-er cry. Break-ing each oth-er's heart. Tear-ing each oth-er a-part.

Repeat and Fade

HONKY CAT

Words and Music by ELTON JOHN
and BERNIE TAUPIN

Brightly, with spirit

(Xylophone)

When I look back, boy, I must have been green,
bop-pin' in the coun-try, fish-in' in a stream.

Copyright © 1972 Dick James Music Limited
All Rights for the United States and Canada Administered by Songs Of PolyGram International, Inc.
International Copyright Secured   All Rights Reserved

D7
Look-in' for an an - swer, try - in' to find a sign,
G
un - til I saw your cit - y lights, hon - ey I was blind. They said,
B7
get back, hon - ky cat, bet - ter get back to the woods well I
E7
quit those days and my red - neck ways and a,
D7
hmm, hmm hmm, hmm, hmm,
oo, oo, oo oo, oo,
oh, the change is gon - na do me good.

G
(Xyl.)
You bet - ter
B7
get back, hon - ky cat liv - in' in the cit - y ain't where it's at, it's like
E7
try'n' to find gold in a sil - ver mine, it's like
D7
To Coda
try'n' to drink whis - key oh, from a bot - tle of wine.
G
(Xyl.)
Well I

D7
read some books and I read some mag - a - zines a - bout those
G
high class la - dies down in New Or - leans and all the
D7
folks back home, well, they said I was a fool. They said,
G
oh, be - lieve in the Lord is the gold - en rule. They said
B7
get back hon - ky cat, Bet - ter get back to the woods, well, I

quit those days_____ and__ my red-neck ways_____ and__
oo,___ oo, oo, oo,__ oo, oh, the change__ is gon-na do me good.__

They said,
They__ said,__ stay__ at home,__ boy, you got-ta tend the farm,__
liv-in' in the cit-y boy,__ is, is gon-na break your heart.__

D7

But how can you stay, when your heart says

G

no, ah, ah, how can you stop when your feet say go.

D.S. al Coda

You bet-ter

CODA

(Xyl.)

D7

Get back, hon-ky cat, get back, hon-ky cat,

G

Repeat and Fade

get back, ooh.

HOPELESSLY DEVOTED TO YOU

Words and Music by
JOHN FARRAR

Moderate 2

Guess mine is not the first _____ heart bro-ken, _____ My
know I'm just a fool _____ who's will-in' _____ to
head is say-in', "Fool, _____ for-get him." _____ My

eyes are not the first _____ to cry. I'm
sit a-round and wait _____ for you. But,
heart is say-in', "Don't _____ let go.

Copyright © 1978 by Unichappell Music, Inc., Ensign Music Corp. and John Farrar Music
All Rights Administered by Unichappell Music, Inc.
International Copyright Secured   All Rights Reserved

Bm6
C#7
Bm6
not the first to know there's just no, get - tin'
ba - by, can't you see there's noth - in' else for
Hold on to the end." And that's what I in -
C#7
1 F#m7
F#
o - ver you.
me to
tend to
G#m7
Gm7
F#m7
B9
2 F#m7
I do
do
G#m7
Gm7
F#m
B13
I'm Hope - less - ly De - vot - ed To

Am E Am E
You. But
cresc.
Dm7
now there's no where to hide since you
f
G7 C
pushed my love a - side. I'm out of my
Edim A7
head, Hope - less - ly De - vot - ed To

You,_____ Hope - less - ly De - vot - ed____ To You._____

My vot - ed____ To You._____

I AM...I SAID

Words and Music by
NEIL DIAMOND

Slowly

L.A.'s fine, the sun shines most the time, and the feelin' is lay back. Palm trees grow, and rents are low. But you know I keep thinkin' 'bout

© 1971, 1974 PROPHET MUSIC, INC.
All Rights Reserved

makin' my way back. Well, I'm New York City born and raised, but nowadays, I'm lost between two shores. L.A.'s fine, but it ain't home. New York's home, but it ain't mine no more.

cresc.

"I am," I said to no one there. And no one heard at all, not even the chair. "I am," I cried. "I am," said I.

And I am lost, and I can't even say why, leavin' me lonely still.

Did you ever read about a frog who dreamed of bein' a king

and then be-came one? _____ Well, ex-cept for the names _____ and a few oth-er chang-es, if you talk a-bout me, _____ the sto-ry's the same one. But I got an emp-ti-ness deep in-side. _____ And I've tried, _____ but it won't let me go.

And I'm not a man who likes to swear, but I've never cared for the sound of bein' alone.

"I am," I

I SHOT THE SHERIFF

Words and Music by
BOB MARLEY

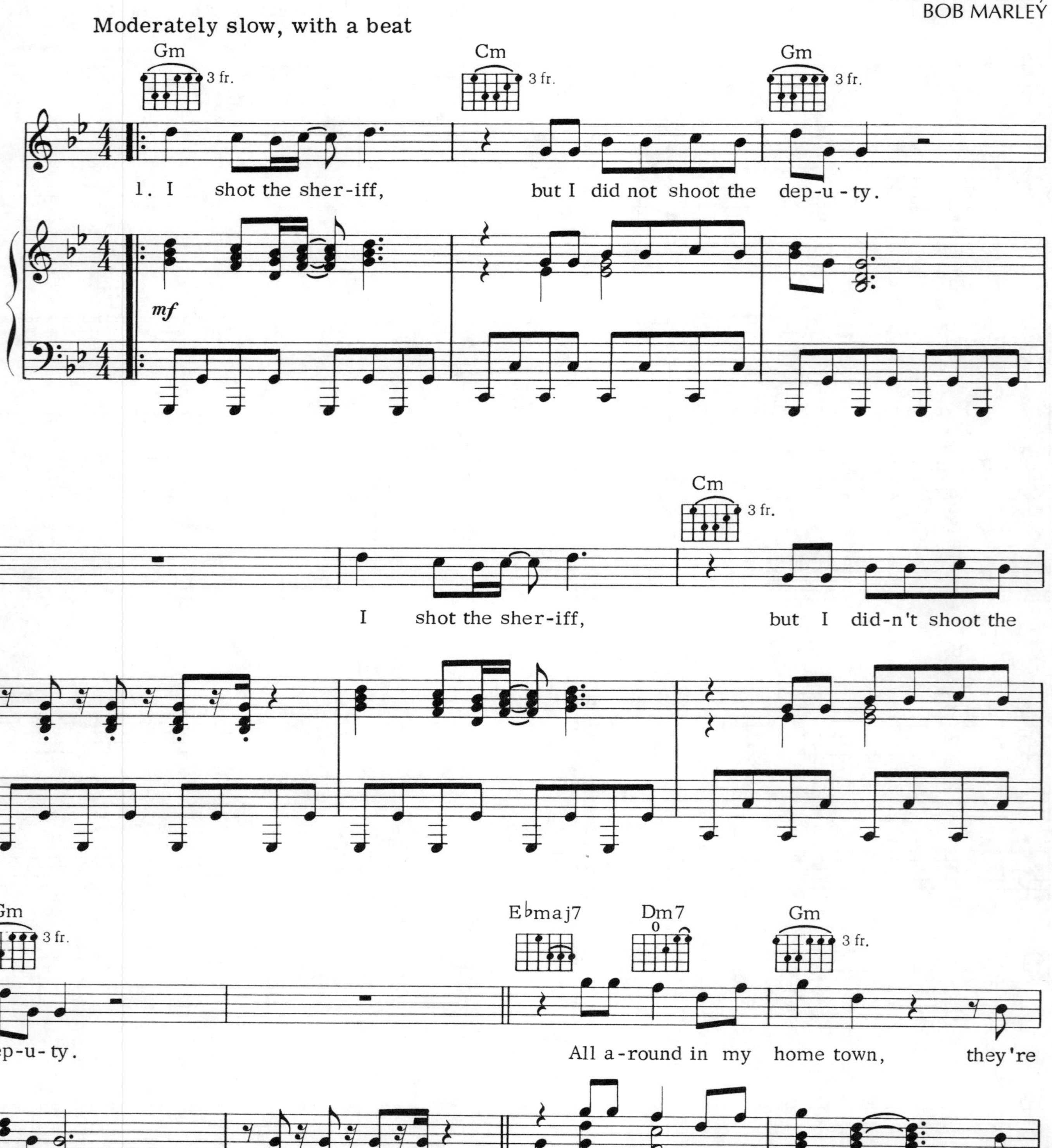

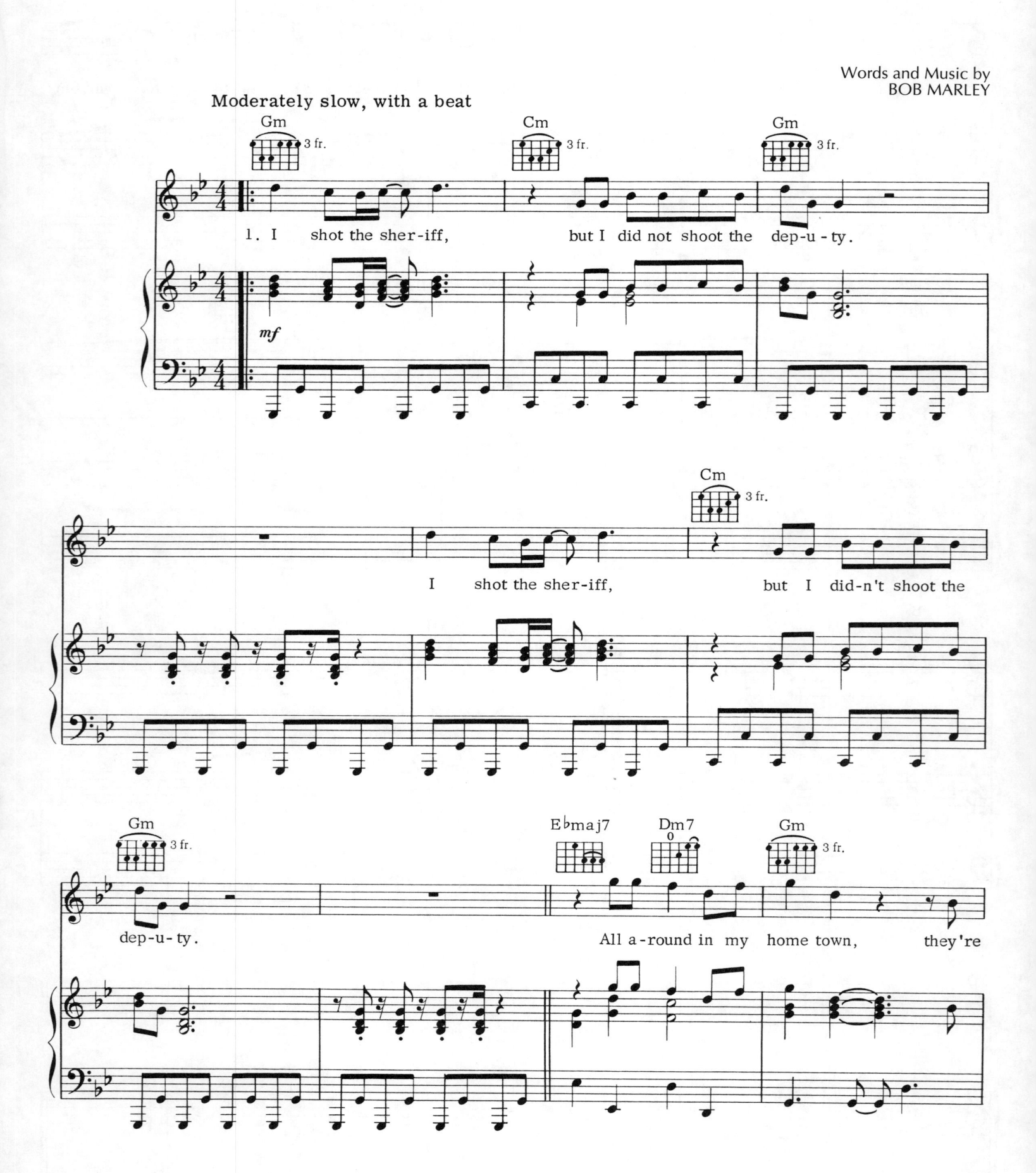

2. I shot the sheriff, but I swear it was in self-defense.
   I shot the sheriff, and they say it is a capital offense.
   Sheriff John Brown always hated me; for what, I don't know.
   Every time that I plant a seed, he said, "Kill it before it grows."
   He said, "Kill it before it grows." But I say:

3. I shot the sheriff, but I swear it was in self-defense.
   I shot the sheriff, but I swear it was in self-defense.
   Freedom came my way one day, and I started out of town.
   All of a sudden, I see sheriff John Brown aiming to shoot me down.
   So I shot, I shot him down. But I say:

4. I shot the sheriff, but I did not shoot the deputy.
   I shot the sheriff, but I didn't shoot the deputy.
   Reflexes got the better of me, and what is to be must be.
   Every day, the bucket goes to the well, but one day the bottom will drop out.
   Yes, one day the bottom will drop out. But I say:

I WRITE THE SONGS

Words and Music by
BRUCE JOHNSTON

*I've been alive forever, and I wrote the very first song.
I put the words and the melodies together, I am*

*My home lies deep within you and I've got my own place in your soul.
Now, when I look out through your eyes I'm*

Copyright © 1970 by Artists Music, Inc.
All Rights Administered by BMG Songs, Inc. (ASCAP)
International Copyright Secured All Rights Reserved

mu - sic, and I write the songs. I write the songs that make the
young a-gain, e-ven though I'm ver-y old.

whole world sing; I write the songs of love and spe - cial things.

I write the songs that make the young girls cry;

I write the songs, I write the songs.

Oh, my music makes you dance and gives you spirit to take a chance, And I wrote some rock 'n' roll so you can move. Music fills your heart, well, that's a real fine place to start, It's from me, it's for you, it's from you, it's for me, it's a world-

Gm7/C C Gm7/C C A Amaj7 Bm7
- wide_ sym-pho-ny._ I write the songs_ that make the whole world sing,
E7 A F#m F#m(#7) F#m7
I write the songs_ of love and spe - cial things,_ I write the songs_ that make the
A/B B7 Bm7/E F#m F#m(#7) F#m7
young girls cry,_ I write the songs_ I write the songs._
A/B B7 Bm7/E A
I am mu - sic and I write the songs.
Ped.

I'M NOT LISA

Words and Music by
JESSI COLTER

Moderately Slow

I'm not Li-sa; my name is Ju-lie. Li-sa left you years a-go. My eyes are not blue, but mine won't leave you 'til the sun-light has touched your face. She *was your morn-ing light, her smile told of no night. Your love for her grew with each ris-ing sun, and then one win-ter day, his hand led her a-way. She left you here drown-ing in your tears, here where you've stayed for years, cry-ing*

B♭
C7
Li - sa, Li - sa. I'm not
F
B♭
Li - sa, my name is Ju - lie; Li - sa
not blue, but mine won't leave you 'til the
C7
1
F
C7
left you years a - go. My eyes are
sun - light
2
F
shines through your face. I'm not Li - sa.
p

IF YOU LEAVE ME NOW

Words and Music by
PETER CETERA

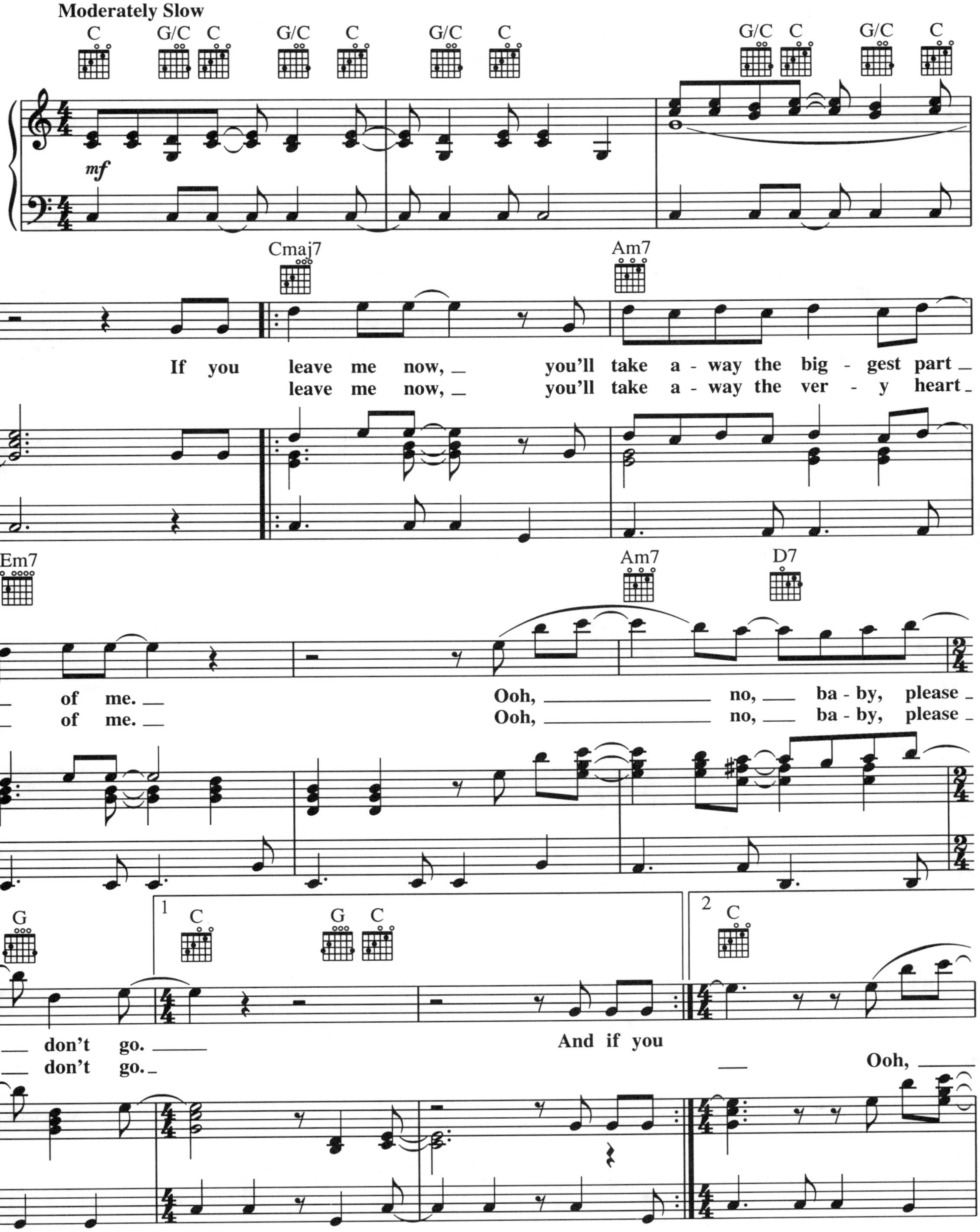

girl, I just want you to stay.

A love like ours is love that's hard to find. How could we let it slip away?
We've come too far to leave it all behind. How could we end it all this way? When to-mor-

row comes, __ then we'll both __ re - gret __ the things we said __ to - day. __

To Coda ⊕

CODA

If you leave me now, you'll take away the biggest part of me. Ooh, no, baby, please don't go.

131

ISLAND GIRL

Words and Music by ELTON JOHN
and BERNIE TAUPIN

With movement

I see your teeth flash Jamaican honey so sweet down where Lexington cross forty seventh street

Oh, she's a big girl, she's standing six foot three

Copyright © 1975 by Big Pig Music Ltd.
Published in the U.S.A. by Intersong-USA, Inc.
International Copyright Secured   All Rights Reserved

turn-ing tricks for the dudes in the big city

Is-land girl what you want-in' wid de white man's world

is-land girl black boy want you in his is-land world.

He want to take you from de rack-et boss. He want to save you but de cause

Eb
Bb
Bb7
Eb
is lost.
Is - land girl,
is - land girl,
is - land girl
C7
Bb/F
To Coda
Eb/G
F7/A
Bb
Guitar Tacet
tell me what you want - in' wid de white man's world.
F
Bb
F
Bb
gliss.
She's
(Instrumental 2nd time.)
Dm
Bb/F
black as coal
but she burn like a fire
C/G
F/A
and she wrap her - self a - round you
like a well worn tire.

Bb
Dm
You feel her nail scratch your back just like a rake,
Bb/F
F
C/G
Oh, he one more gone, he one more john who make
Ab
Eb
Ab
Eb
D.S. al Coda
de mis-take
Is-land
Is-land
CODA
Eb/G
F7/A
white man's
Bb/F
Eb/G
F7/A
F
Bb/F
Tell me what you want-in' wid de white man's
gliss.
F
Bb/F
F
Bb/F
gliss.

IT'S IMPOSSIBLE
(SOMOS NOVIOS)

English Lyric by SID WAYNE
Spanish Words and Music by ARMANDO MANZANERO

Slowly, with expression

It's im-pos-si-ble, tell the sun to leave the sky, it's just im-pos-si-ble.
So-mos no-vios pues los dos sen-ti-mos mu tuo a-mor pro-fun-do

It's im-pos-si-ble, ask a
Y con e-so ya ga-

Copyright © 1968 by BMG Edim., S.A. De C.V.
All Rights for the U.S.A. Administered by BMG Songs, Inc.
International Copyright Secured   All Rights Reserved

| Dm7 | G7 | Bm7♭5 |

ba - by not to cry, it's just im - pos - si - ble.
na - mos lo más gran - de de es - te mun - do.

| E7 | Am7 | Cm |

Can I hold you ___ clos - er to me, ___ and not
Nos a - ma - mos ___ nos be - sa - mos ___ co - mo

| G | E7♭9 | Am |

feel you ___ go - ing through me? ___ Split the sec - ond ___ that I
no - vios ___ nos de - se - a - mos y has - ta a ve - ces ___ sin mo -

| A7 | D7 |

nev - er think of you? Oh, how im - pos - si - ble.
ti - vo sin ra - zón nos e - no - ja - mos.

Am7 D7 G G6 Gmaj7 G6
Can the o - cean keep from rush-ing to the shore? It's just im -
So - mos no - vios man - te - ne - mos un ca - ri - ño lim - pio y
F♯m7♭5 B7 Em
pos - si - ble. If I had you, could I
pu - ro. Co - mo to - dos pro - cu -
Dm7 G7 Bm7♭5 E7
ev - er want for more? It's just im - pos - si - ble. And to -
ra - mos el mo - men - to más os - cu - ro pa - ra ha -
Am7 Cm
mor - row, should you ask me for the world, some - how I'd
blar - nos pa - ra dar - nos el más dul - ce de los

G
E7♭9
get it. I would sell my ver - y soul and not re -
be - sos re - cor - dar de que co - lor son los ce -
Am
D7
1 G
gret it, for to live with-out your love is just im - pos - si - ble.
re - zos Sin ha - cer más co - men - ta - rios so - mos no - vios.
C♯m7♭5
D7
no chord
2 G
Em7
It's im - pos - si - ble. Im - pos - si - ble.
So - mos no - vios somos no - vios
Am7
D7
G
Cm6
G
Mm, im - pos - si - ble.
siem - pre no - vios.
rall.

The Last Time I Felt Like This

from SAME TIME, NEXT YEAR

Words by ALAN BERGMAN and MARILYN BERGMAN
Music by MARVIN HAMLISCH

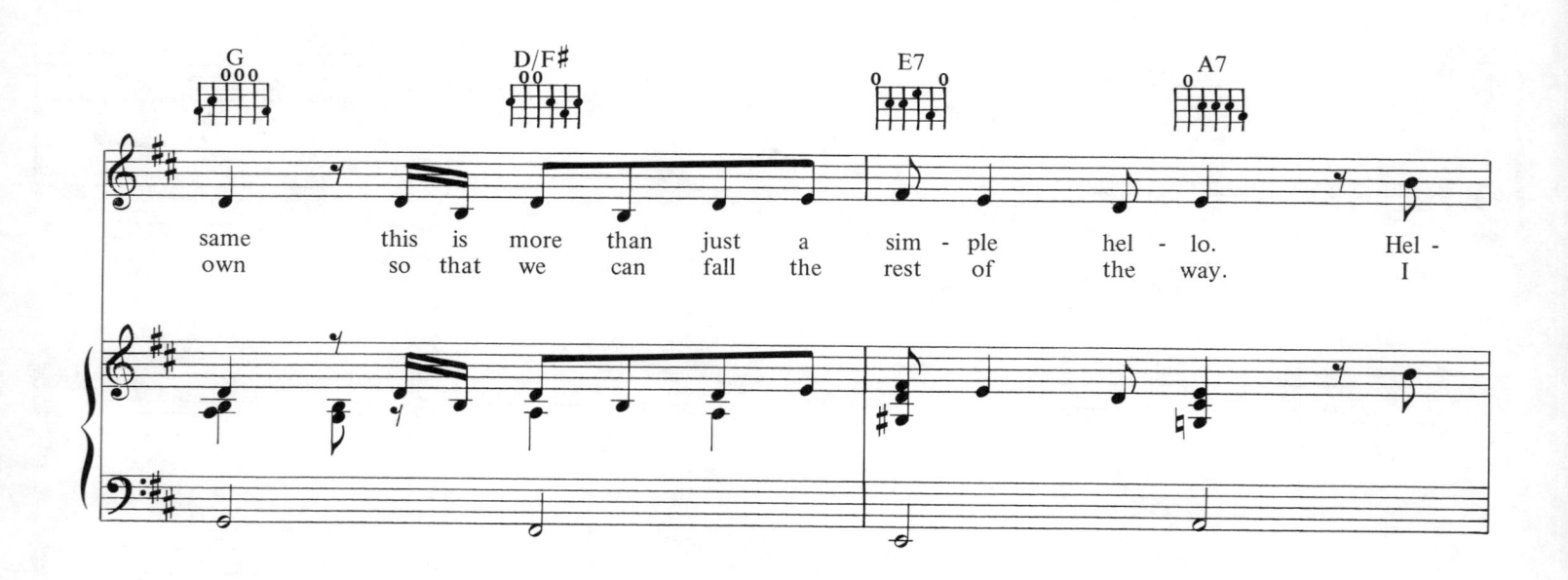

Slow Ballad tempo

Hel - lo, I don't_ e - ven know_ your name, but I'm hop - in' all_ the
lo, I can't_ wait till we're_ a - lone, some - where qui - et on_ our

same this is more than just a sim - ple hel - lo. Hel -
own so that we can just fall the rest of the way. I

© Copyright 1978 by ON BACKSTREET MUSIC, INC.
ON BACKSTREET MUSIC, INC. is an MCA Company
International Copyright Secured   All Rights Reserved

MCA music publishing

D A/C♯ Bm7 D/A
lo, do I smile and walk a - way? No, I think I'll smile and
know that be - fore the night is thru, I'll be talk - ing love to
G D/F♯ Em7 A7 G A/G
stay to see where this might go.
you, mean - ing ev - 'ry word I say.
'Cause the last time I felt like this
F♯m7 Bm G Gmaj7/A A7 G A D/F♯
I was fall - ing in love, fall - ing and feel - ing I'd nev - er fall in love a - gain. Yes, the
G A/G F♯m7 Bm 1. G G/A A7
last time I felt like this was long be - fore I knew what I'm feel - ing now with

D Gmaj7 D Gmaj7/A
2. G G/A A7
you. Hel- feel - ing now with
Repeat and fade
D G D/F♯ Em7 D G A/G F♯m7 Bm
you. Oh, the last time I felt like this I was fall - ing in love,
G Gmaj7/A A7 G A D/F♯ G A/G
fall - ing and feel - ing _ I'd nev - er fall in love a - gain. Yes, the last time I felt like this,
F♯m7 Bm G G/A A7 D G D/F♯ Em7 D
was long be - fore I knew _ what I'm feel - ing now with you. Oh, the

MAGGIE MAY

Words and Music by ROD STEWART
and MARTIN QUITTENTON

Moderately bright

Wake up, Mag-gie, I think I got some-thing to say to you: It's late Sep-tem-ber and I real-ly should be back at school. I know I keep you a-mused, but I feel I'm be-ing used, Oh,

Em F#m Em7
Mag - gie, I could - n't have tried any - y more. You
Em A Em A
lured me a - way from home, just to save you from be - ing a - lone. You
Em A D
stole my heart and that's what real - ly hurts. The
A G D
morn - ing sun, when it's in your face, real - ly shows your age, But
A G D G
that don't wor - ry me none in my eyes you're ev - 'ry - thing. I laughed at all of your

2. You lured me away from home, just to save you from being alone.
You stole my soul, that's a pain I can do without.
All I needed was a friend to lend a guiding hand.
But you turned into a lover, and, Mother, what a lover! You wore me out.
All you did was wreck my bed, and in the morning kick me in the head.
Oh, Maggie, I couldn't have tried any more.

3. You lured me away from home, 'cause you didn't want to be alone.
You stole my heart, I couldn't leave you if I tried.
I suppose I could collect my books and get back to school.
Or steal my Daddy's cue and make a living out of playing pool,
Or find myself a rock and roll band that needs a helpin' hand.
Oh, Maggie, I wish I'd never seen your face. **(To Coda)**

MAYBE I'M AMAZED

Words and Music by
PAUL McCARTNEY

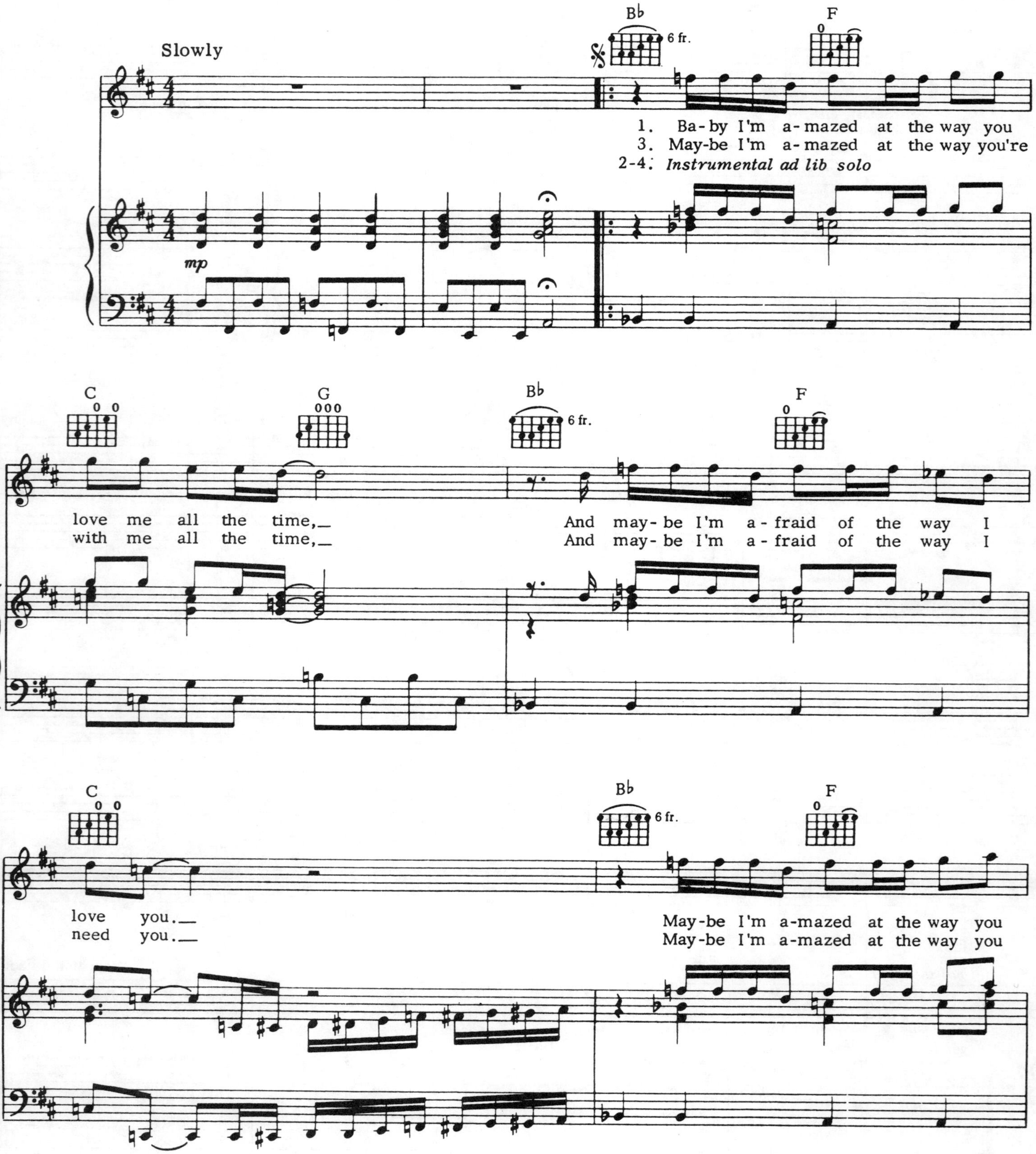

pulled me out of time,___ hung me on a line,___ And
help me sing my song,___ right me when I'm wrong,___

may-be I'm a-mazed at the way I real-ly need you.___

4th time to Coda ⊕

Ba-by, I'm a man, may-be I'm a lone-ly man_ who's in the mid-dle of some-thing_

that he does-n't real-ly un-der-stand.___

Ba-by, I'm a man, and may-be you're the on-ly wom-an who could ev-er help me;

Ba-by, won't you help me to un-der-stand? Oo

D.S. al Coda

3rd time rit.

Coda

(Keep repeating with ad lib guitar figures till fade)

ME AND YOU AND A DOG NAMED BOO

Words and Music by
LOBO

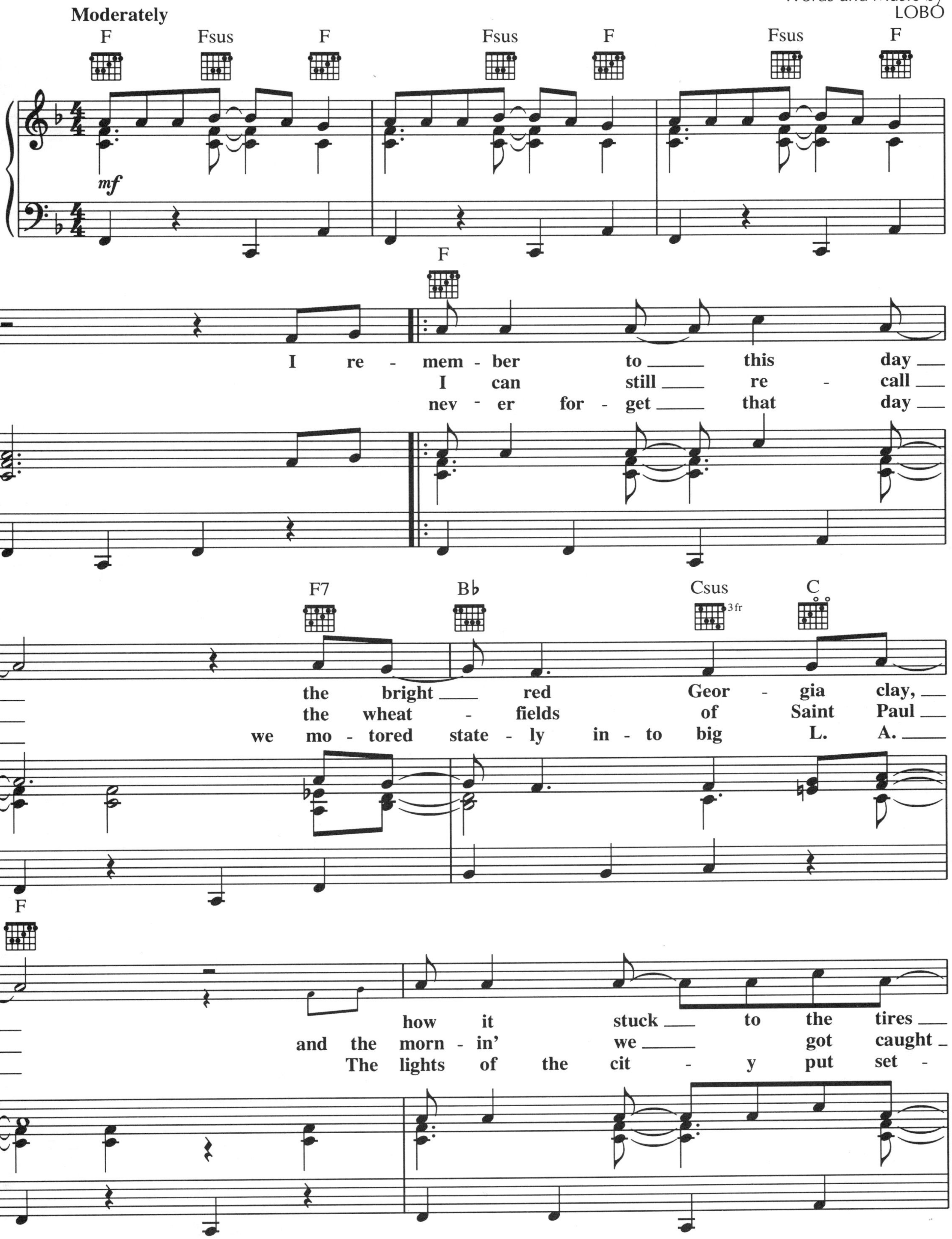

C
Csus
3 fr
after the summer rain. Will-
robbin' from an old hen. Old Mac-
-tlin' down in my brain. Though it's
F
F7
power made that old car go, A woman's
Donald, he made us work, But then he
only been a month or so, That old car's
B♭
Csus
3 fr
C
F
mind told me that it's so.
paid us for what it was worth. An-
buggin' us to go. You
E♭
3 fr
B♭
C
Oh, how I wish we were back on the road again.
other tank of gas and back on the road again.
gotta get away and get back on the road again.

Me and you and a dog named Boo, trav-el-in' and liv-in' off the land. Me and you and a dog named Boo, how I love be-in' a free man.

2.
3. I'll

NEITHER ONE OF US
(WANTS TO BE THE FIRST TO SAY GOODBYE)

Words and Music by
JIM WEATHERLY

It's sad to think we're not gonna make it, and it's gotten to the point where we just can't fake it, but for

Copyright © 1971 PolyGram International Publishing, Inc.
International Copyright Secured   All Rights Reserved

some un-god-ly rea-son, we just won't let it die. I guess nei-ther one of us wants to be the first to say good-bye. I keep won-d'ring what I'll do with-out you. And I *guess you must be wondering that same thing too.*

So we go on together, living a lie, because neither one of us wants to be the first to say good-bye.

B♭
Fmaj7
Ev-'ry-time I find the nerve to say I'm leav-in',
Gm
Gm7/C
old mem-o-ries get in the
Fmaj7
F7
B♭
way.
Lord knows it's on-ly me
Am
that I'm de-ceiv-ing;
When it

comes to say-ing good-bye, that's a word I just can't say. There can be no way this can have a hap-py end-ing. So we just go on hurt-ing and pre-tend-ing, And con-

B♭
Am7
B♭
vinc - ing our - selves to give it just one more try.
B♭m
F/C
C7
Be-cause nei-ther one of us wants to be the one to say good-
Dm
Dm/C
G7
F/C
bye;
Be-cause nei - ther one of us
C7
F
B♭
F
wants to be the first to say good - bye.
rit.

NIGHT FEVER
(From "SATURDAY NIGHT FEVER")

Words and Music by BARRY GIBB,
MAURICE GIBB and ROBIN GIBB

Medium Rock beat

Lis-ten to the ground: there is move-ment all a-round. There is
heat of our love, don't need no help for us to make it. Gim-me

some-thing go-in' down, and I can feel it. On the
just e-nough to take us to the morn-in'. I got

Copyright © 1977 by Gibb Brothers Music
All Rights Administered by Careers-BMG Music Publishing, Inc.
International Copyright Secured   All Rights Reserved

Dm
waves of the air, there is danc - in' out there. If it's
fire in my mind. I got high - er in my walk - in'. And I'm
F
Bb
C
some - thin' we can share, we can steal it.
glow - in' in the dark; I give you warn - in'.
And that
Am
Bb
sweet cit - y wom - an, she moves through the light, con -
Am
Em
trol - ling my mind and my soul. When you

Am
Dm
A
reach out for me, yeah, and the feel - in' is bright, then I get
Dm7
Gm7
3 fr.
night fe - ver, night fe - ver. We know how to do
Fmaj7
Gm7
3 fr.
it. Gim - me that
Dm7
Gm7
3 fr.
night fe - ver, night fe - ver. We know how to show

— it.

Here I am, prayin' for this moment to last, livin' on the music so fine, borne on the wind, makin' it mine.

Dm7
Gm7
3 fr.
Night fe - ver, night fe - ver. We know how to do
Fmaj7
Gm7
3 fr.
it. Gim - me that
Dm7
Gm7
3 fr.
Fmaj7
night fe - ver, night fe - ver. We know how to show it.
1.
Gm7
3 fr.
In the
2.
Gm7
3 fr.
D. S. 𝄋 and fade
Gim - me that

ONE TIN SOLDIER

Words and Music by DENNIS LAMBERT
and BRIAN POTTER

Moderately slow rock tempo

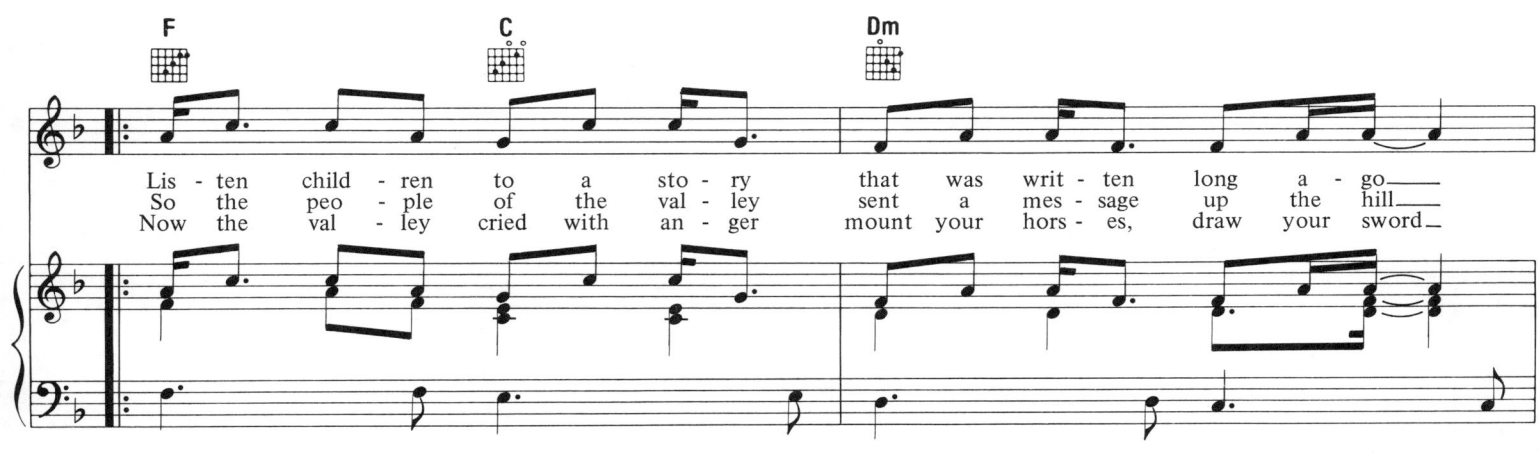

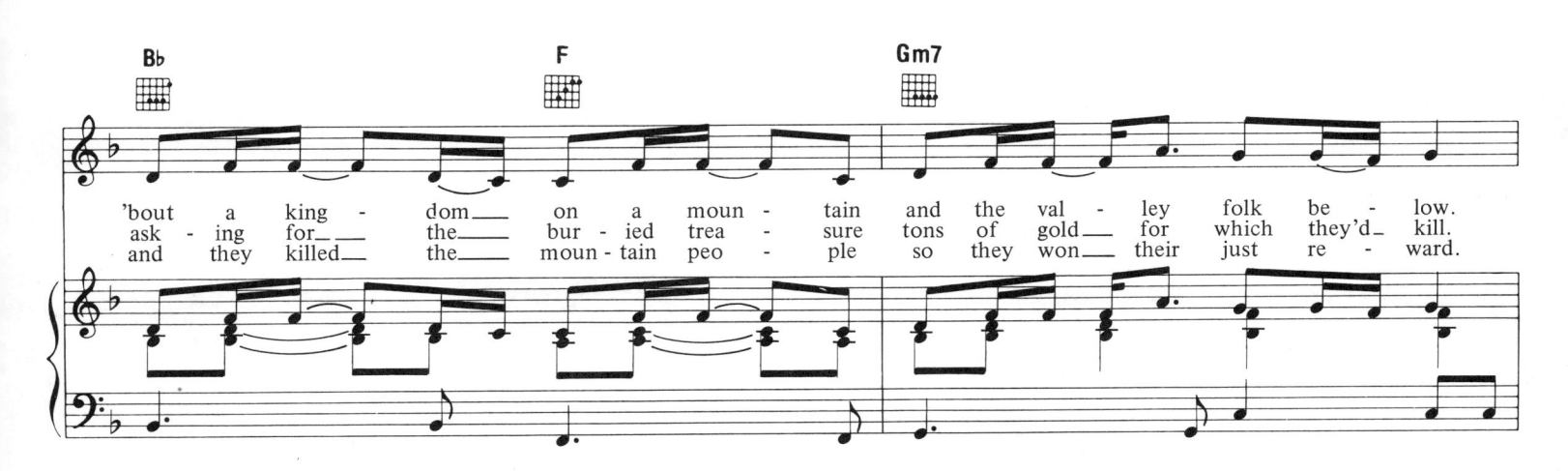

Listen children to a story that was written long ago
So the people of the valley sent a message up the hill
Now the valley cried with anger mount your horses, draw your sword

'bout a kingdom on a mountain and the valley folk below.
asking for the buried treasure tons of gold for which they'd kill.
and they killed the mountain people so they won their just reward.

© Copyright 1969, 1974 by DUCHESS MUSIC CORPORATION
DUCHESS MUSIC CORPORATION is an MCA Company
International Copyright Secured   All Rights Reserved

MCA music publishing

On the moun-tain was a trea-sure bur-ied deep be-neath a stone
Came an an-swer from the king-dom "With our broth-ers we will share
Now they stood be-side the trea-sure on the moun-tain, dark and red

and the val-ley peo-ple swore they'd have it for their ver-y
all the se-crets of our moun-tain, all the rich-es bur-ied
turned the stone and looked be-neath it "Peace on earth" was all it

own.
there."
said.

Go a-head and hate your neigh-bor,

go a-head and cheat a friend. Do it in the name of hea-ven

Jus - ti - fy it in the end. There won't be an - y trum - pets blow - in'
come the judge - ment day on the blood - y morn - ing af - ter
one tin sold - ier rides a - way.

ONE TOKE OVER THE LINE

Words and Music by MICHAEL BREWER
and THOMAS E. SHIPLEY

Moderate Country

One toke o-ver the line, ___ sweet Je-sus, one toke o-ver the line. ___

Copyright © 1970 by Careers-BMG Music Publishing, Inc.
International Copyright Secured   All Rights Reserved

Sit-tin' down-town in a rail-way sta-tion, one toke o-ver the line. Wait-in' for the train that goes home, sweet Ma-ry, hop-in' that the train is on time. Sit-tin' down-town in a rail-way sta-tion,

one toke o-ver the line.
Who do you / I sailed a-
love? / way
I hope it's me. / a coun-try mile
I've been chang-in', / and now I'm re-turn-in',
as you can plain-ly see. / show-in' off my smile.
I felt the joy and I / I met all the girls and I

169

learned a-bout the pain _____ that my ma-ma said. _____
loved my-self a few, _____ when to my sur-prise _____

If I should choose to make a part of me, _____
like ev-'ry-thing else that I've been through, _____

would sure-ly strike me dead. ___ And now I'm
it o-pened up my eyes. ___ And now I'm

D.S. al Coda

CODA
___ One ___ toke, one toke o-ver the line. ___

PIECES OF APRIL

Words and Music by
DAVE LOGGINS

Moderately

Verse

A-pril gave us Spring-time, And a prom-ise of the flow-ers;

And a feel-ing that we both shared, And a love that we called ours.

And we knew no time for sad-ness, That's a road we each had crossed.

© Copyright 1972 by MCA MUSIC PUBLISHING, A Division of MCA INC. and POLYGRAM INTERNATIONAL PUBLISHING, INC.
All Rights Administered by MCA MUSIC PUBLISHING, A Division of MCA INC.
International Copyright Secured   All Rights Reserved

And we were liv-ing a time meant for us, And e-ven when it would rain, we'd laugh it off.

Chorus

And I've got piec - es of A - pril that I keep in a mem - o - ry bou - quet. I've got piec - es of A - pril, And it's a morn-ing in May.

Fine

We stood on the crest of summer, beneath a oak of blossomed green;
Feelin' as I did in April; Not really knowin' just what it means;
But it must be then that stands beside me now, to make me feel this way;
Just as I did in April, and it's a mornin' in May.

D.S. al Fine

Please Come to Boston

Words and Music by
DAVE LOGGINS

Moderato

Verse

1. Please come to Bos-ton for the spring-time. I'm stay-ing here with some friends and they've got lots of room. You can sell your paint-ings on the side-walk, by a ca-fé where I

2. Please come to Den-ver with the snow-fall. We'll move up in-to the moun-tains so far that we can't be found and throw 'I love you' ech-o's down the can-yons. And then lie a-wake at

© Copyright 1972 by MCA MUSIC PUBLISHING, A Division of MCA INC. and POLYGRAM INTERNATIONAL PUBLISHING, INC.
Rights Administered by MCA MUSIC PUBLISHING, A Division of MCA INC.
International Copyright Secured   All Rights Reserved

MCA music publishing

hope to be working soon. Please come to {Boston, Denver, L.A.} she said no, but
night un-til they come back a-round

you come home to me. And she said hey ram-blin' boy, now won't you set-tle down

{Boston, Denver, L.A.} ain't your kind of town There ain't no gold and there ain't no-bod-y like

me I'm the num-ber one fan of the man from Ten-nes-see

ADDITIONAL LYRICS

Verse 3.
    Please come to L.A. to live forever
    A California life alone is just too hard to build
    I live in a house that looks out over the ocean
    And there's some stars that fell from the sky
    Living up on the hill
    Please come to L.A., she just said no,
    Boy, won't you come home to me.
Repeat Chorus

PRECIOUS AND FEW

Words and Music by
WALTER D. NIMS

Moderately

Pre-cious and few ___ are the mo-ments we two can share.
Ba-by it's you ___ on my mind, ___ your love is so rare.

Qui-et and blue like the sky ___
Be-ing with you ___ is a feel-

___ I'm hung o-ver you. ___ And if I
-ing I just can't com-pare. ___ And if I

Copyright © 1970, 1972 by Famous Music Corporation and Emerald City Music
All Rights for the World Controlled and Administered by Famous Music Corporation
International Copyright Secured   All Rights Reserved

can't find my way back home
can't hold you in my arms

it just would-n't be fair,

'cause pre-cious and few are the mo-ments we two can

share.

share.

F
F7
E♭maj7
Am7
D7
3
And if I can't find my way back home
Gm7
C7
Fmaj7
E♭
B♭/D
it just would - n't be fair,
'cause pre-cious and few are the mo -
Cm7
F7
B♭
B♭/A♭
F♯7
- ments we two can share.
B
C♯m7
A
F♯
Pre-cious and few are the mo - ments we two can share.

B
C#m7
4fr
A
F#
F#7
Quiet and blue like the sky I'm hung over you.
And if I
Emaj7
Bbm7
Eb7
G#m7
4fr
C#7
can't find my way back home
it just wouldn't be fair,
F#maj7
E
B/D#
4fr
C#m7
4fr
F#7
E
B/D#
4fr
'cause precious and few are the moments we two can share.
F#7
B
C#m7/B
4fr
Bdim
B
rit.

READY TO TAKE A CHANCE AGAIN
(Love Theme)
(From The Paramount Picture "FOUL PLAY")

Words by NORMAN GIMBEL
Music by CHARLES FOX

Moderately

You remind me I live in a shell, safe from the past, and doin' o-kay, but not ver-y well.

Copyright © 1977, 1978 by Ensign Music Corporation and Kamakazi Music Corporation
All Rights for the World Controlled and Administered by Ensign Music Corporation
International Copyright Secured   All Rights Reserved

No jolts, no surprises, no crisis arises. My life goes along as it should, it's all very nice, but

| Dm/B | | Dm/E | E7♭9 | Am7 |

not ver-y good._____ And I'm read-y to take_ a chance_

rall. *a tempo*

| Dm7 | F/G | G/F | C/E | Am/E | E7/G# |

_ a-gain,_ read-y to put_ my love_ on the line_ with

| Am | Am/G | G♭7♭5 | Fmaj7 | Em7 | Dm7 | Em7 |

you. Been liv-ing with noth-ing to show_ for it._ You

| Dm7 | F/G | G/F | C/E | Fmaj7 |

To Coda ⊕

get what you get_ when you go_ for it,_ and I'm read-y to take_ a chance_

E/G#
a - gain with you.
Am
E/G#
A/G
When she left me in all my de - spair,
A7
Dm
Dm/C
I just held on. My hopes were all gone, then
Dm/B
Dm/E
D.S. al Coda
E7♭9
I found you there. And I'm
CODA
C/E
Fmaj7
read - y to take a chance

F♯m7♭5
4fr
C/G
E/G♯
a - gain, ready - y to take a chance a - gain with you,
Am7
with you.
Dm7
F/G
G/F
C/E
Am/E
E7/G♯
Repeat ad lib. and Fade
Am7
Dm7
F/G
G/F
C/E
Am/E
E7/G♯

Right Time of the Night

Words and Music by
PETER McCANN

Moderate

1.) Sun goes down on a silk-y day; quar-ter moon walk-in' thru the Milk-y Way. Oh, you and me ba-by, we could think of some-thin' to do.

2.) No use talk-ing when the sha-dows fall; night birds call-ing and he says it all.

It's the

© Copyright 1976, 1977 by MCA MUSIC PUBLISHING, A Division of MCA INC.
International Copyright Secured   All Rights Reserved
MCA music publishing

right time of the night; the stars are wink-in' a-bove. It's the right time of the night for mak-in' love.

I got you and you got me; tell you that's the way my mom-ma al-ways said it should be. I'll be good,

D♭
D♭
(E♭ Bass)
D.S. al Coda
you be kind; we'll be bad if you don't mind. It's the
Coda
Bm7
D
(E Bass)
A
C♯m7
D
D
(E Bass)
It's the right time of the night;
A
C♯m7
D
D
(E Bass)
A
C♯m7
the stars are wink - in' a - bove. It's the right time of the
D
D
(E Bass)
A
D
(E Bass)
A
D
(E Bass)
Repeat and Fade
night for mak - in' love. It's the

THE ROCKFORD FILES
(Theme From The Universal Television Series "THE ROCKFORD FILES")

Music by MIKE POST
and PETE CARPENTER

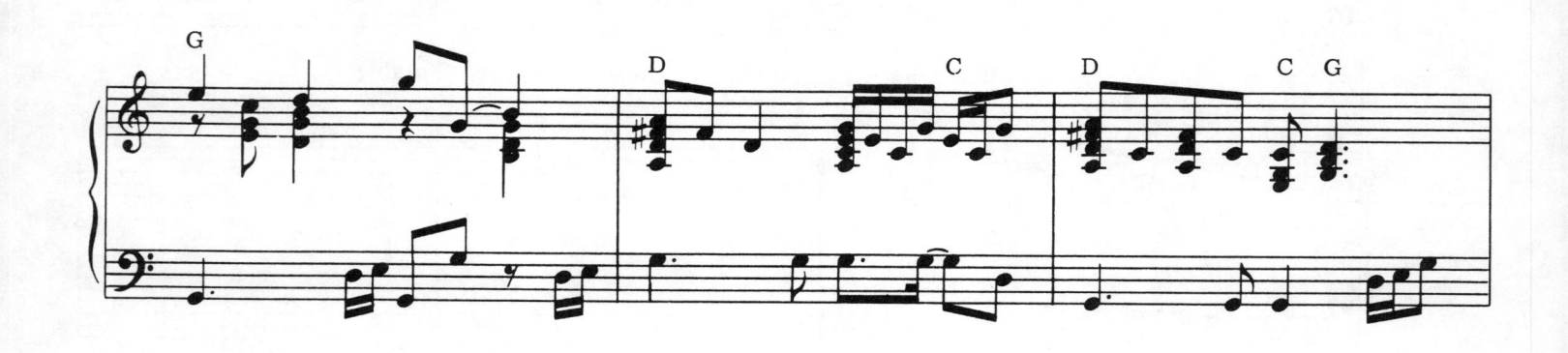

G
C
G
G
D
C
D
C
G
Em
Eb+
G/D
Dbm7(b5)
C
B7(sus)
B7
Em
Eb+
G/D
Dbm7(b5)
Am7
B7
C
C#dim
D7(sus)
G

SAD EYES

Words and Music by
ROBERT JOHN PEDRICK

Looks like it's o - ver, you knew I ___ could-n't stay. ___ She's com-in' home to day. ___ We had a good thing. ___ I'll

Try to re-mem-ber the mag-ic ___ that we shared. ___ In time your bro-ken heart will mend. ___ I nev-er used you. ___ You

Copyright © 1979 by Careers-BMG Music Publishing, Inc. and Chappell & Co.
International Copyright Secured   All Rights Reserved

Dm7/C
F/C
miss your sweet love.
Why must you look at me that
knew I real - ly cared.
I hate to see it have to
G
Gsus
G
Dm7
F
way?
It's o - ver.
end,
but it's o - ver.
C
G/C
Dm9
Dm7
1.,2. Sad eyes,
turn the oth - er way.
3. Instrumental solo
F
C
F/G
I don't wan - na see
you cry.

C
G/C
Dm9
Dm7
Sad ______ eyes, you knew there'd _ come a day when
F
To Coda
1
C
F/G
we would _ have to say good - bye. ____
2
C
F/G
D.S. al Coda
bye. ____
CODA
C
F/G
Solo ends
C
G/C
Dm9
Dm7
Sad ______ eyes, you knew there'd _ come a day when

F C G/A D A/D
we would have to say good - bye.
Sad eyes,
Em9 Em7 G
turn the oth - er way.
I don't wan - na see you
D G/A D A/D Em9 Em7
cry.
Sad eyes,
you knew there'd come a day when
G D G/A
Repeat and Fade
we would have to say good - bye.

SHE BELIEVES IN ME

Words and Music by
STEVE GIBB

Slowly with movement

While she lays sleeping, I stay out late at night and play my songs, And sometimes all the nights can be so long, And it's good when I fin-'ly make it home all a-lone. While she lays

Copyright © 1977 PolyGram International Publishing, Inc.
International Copyright Secured   All Rights Reserved

Bb
Bb7/D
Eb
Bb/D
dream - ing I try to get un - dressed with - out the light. Then
Cm7
F7
F/Eb
Dm7
Gm7
qui - et - ly she says, "How was your night?" And I come to her and say it was all
Cm
F7
Bb
F7sus
right. And I hold her tight. And she be -
Bbsus
Bb
Bbsus
Bb
Am7-5
lieves in me. I'll nev - er know just what she sees in me.

D7 Gm Gm(+7) Gm7 Gm6
I told her some-day if she was my girl I could change the world with my
Cm7 F7sus B♭sus B♭
lit-tle songs, I was wrong. But she has faith in me,
B♭sus B♭ Am7-5 D7
And so I go on try-ing faith-ful-ly, And who knows, may-be on some
Gm Gm(+7) Gm7 Gm6 Cm7
spe-cial night If my song is right I will find a way,

F7sus
Bb
Bb/D
find a way. While she lays wait-ing I stum-ble to the kit-chen for a
Eb
Cm7
F7
F/Eb
Dm7
bite. Then I see my old gui-tar in the night, just
Gm7
Cm7
F7sus
wait-ing for me like a sec-ret friend, And there's no end. While she lays
Bb
Bb7/D
Eb
Bb/D
cry-ing I fum-ble with a mel-o-dy or two, Then I'm

torn be-tween the things that I should do. Then she says to wake her up___ when I am through___ God, her love is true___ And she be-lieves in me, I'll nev-er know just what she sees___ in me.___ I told her some-day___ if she was my girl___ I could change the world___ with my lit-tle songs,___ I was

F7sus
Bbsus
Bb
Bbsus
Bb
wrong. But she has faith in me, And so I go on try-ing
Am7-5
D7
Gm
Gm(+7)
faith-ful-ly, And who knows, may-be on some spe-cial night If my
Gm7
Gm6
Cm7
F7sus
song is right I will find a way, while she
Bb
Eb/Bb
Ebm
Bb
waits, while she waits, for me.

SPEAK SOFTLY, LOVE
(LOVE THEME)
(From The Paramount Picture "THE GODFATHER")

Words by LARRY KUSIK
Music by NINO ROTA

Speak softly, love, and hold me warm against your heart. I feel your words, the tender, trembling moments start. We're in a world our very own, sharing a love that only few have ever known. Wine colored

Copyright © 1972 by Famous Music Corporation
International Copyright Secured   All Rights Reserved

Bb7/D
Bb7
Eb
3fr
Db/F
Fm6/Ab
6fr
days warmed by the sun, deep vel-vet nights when we are
G
no chord
Cm
Fm/C
one. Speak soft-ly, love, so no one hears us but the sky. The vows of
Fm/C
Cm
Fm6/C
Cm
Fm/C
Fm
love we make will live un-til we die. My life is yours and all be-
Cm
Cm/G
G7sus
G7
1
2
cause you came in-to my world with love so soft-ly, love. Speak soft-ly, love.
rit.

SHE'S ALWAYS A WOMAN

Words and Music by
BILLY JOEL

Eb Ebsus Eb Bb Eb Bb
me. She can lead you to love, she can take you or
Eb Ab Abmaj7
leave you she can ask for the truth but she'll nev - er be -
Ab6 Ab Bb7 Eb Bb7 G
lieve you, And she'll take what you give her as long as it's free yeah, she
Cm Cm Bb bass Ab6 Bb7 Eb Ebsus Eb Eb D bass
steals like a thief but she's al-ways a wom-an to me.

Cm
Cm
Bbbass
F7
A bass
F7
Bb
Bb
A bass
Gm
Eb
Oh she takes care of her-self she can wait if she
Ab
Ab
G bass
Fm
Bb7
Eb
Ab
Ebbass
Eb
wants, she's a-head of her time.
Ebm
Ebm
Db bass
Cm
Ab
Db
Db
C bass
Bbm
Gb6
Oh and she nev-er gives out and she nev-er gives
Cb
Cb
Bbbass
Adim7
F7
Bb
Bb6
Bb7
in, she just chang-es her mind.
1. And she'll prom-ise you
2. She is fre-quent-ly

Eb
Bb
Eb
Eb7
more than the gar - den of E - den. Then she'll care-less - ly
kind and she's sud - den - ly cru - el. She can do as she
Ab
Abmaj7
Ab6
Ab
Bb7
cut you and laugh while you're bleed - in'. But she brings out the
pleas - es she's no - bo - dy's fool But she can't be con -
Eb
Bb7
G
To Coda
Cm
Cm
Bbbass
Ab6
Bb7
best and the worst you can be Blame it all on your-self cause she's al-ways a wom-an to
vict-ed she's earned her de-gree. And the
Eb
Ebsus
Eb
Bb
Eb
Bb
G
me.
(Hum)
(Hum)

most she will do is throw sha-dows at you But she's al-ways a wom-an to me. (Hum) (Hum)

YEAR OF THE CAT

Words and Music by IAN ALASTIR STEWART
and PETER WOOD

On a morn-ing from a Bo-gart mov-ie, in a coun-try where they turned back time, you go stroll-ing through the crowd like

does-n't give you time for ques-tions as she locks up your arm in hers. And you fol-low till your sense of

morn-ing comes and you're still with her and the bus and the tour-ists are gone. And you've thrown a-way your choice and

Copyright © 1976 Dick James Music Ltd. and Chappell & Co. Ltd.
All Rights for Dick James Music Ltd. in the United States and Canada Administered by Songs Of PolyGram International, Inc.
All Rights for Chappell & Co. Ltd. in the United States and Canada Administered by Chappell & Co.
International Copyright Secured   All Rights Reserved

Pe - ter Lor - re con - tem - plat - ing a crime. She comes
which di - rec - tion com - plete - ly dis - ap - pears. By the
lost your tick - et so you have to stay on. But the

out of the sun in a silk dress, run - ning like a
blue - tiled walls near the mar - ket stalls, there's a
drum - beat strains of the night re main in the

wa - ter - col - or in the rain. Don't both - er ask - ing for
hid - den door she leads you to. "These days," she says, "I
rhy - thm of the new - born day. You know some - time you're

ex - plan - a - tions. She'll just tell you that she came in the year of the cat.
feel my life just like a riv - er run - ning through the year of the cat."
bound to leave her, but for now you're gon - na stay in the year of the cat.

She

Well, she

B
C
looks at you so cool - ly and her
G
D
B
eyes shine like the moon in the sea. She comes in in - cense and patch -
C
G
F6
C/E
ou - li. So you take her to find what's wait - ing in - side
D
Cmaj7
D6
Em
the year of the cat.

Well,

Repeat and Fade

WHERE DO I BEGIN
(LOVE THEME)
(From The Paramount Picture "LOVE STORY")

Words by CARL SIGMAN
Music by FRANCIS LAI

Slowly

With pedal

Where do I be-gin _____ to tell the sto-ry of how
With her first hel-lo _____ she gave a mean-ing to this

great a love can be, _____ the sweet love sto-ry that is
emp-ty world of mine. _____ There'd nev-er be an-oth-er

old-er than the sea, the sim-ple truth a-bout the
love, an-oth-er time; she came in-to my life and

Copyright © 1970, 1971 by Famous Music Corporation
International Copyright Secured   All Rights Reserved

love she brings to me? ____ Where do I start?
made the liv-ing fine. ____

She fills my heart. ____

She fills my heart ____ with ver-y spe-cial things, ____ with an-gel songs, ____ with wild i-mag-in-ings. ____ She fills my soul ____ with so much

love that an-y-where I go I'm nev-er lone-ly. With her a-long, who could be lone-ly? I reach for her hand, it's al-ways there. How long does it last? Can love be meas-ured by the hours in a day? I have no answers now, but this much I can say:

I know I'll need her 'til the stars all burn a-way, and she'll be

there.

WISHING YOU WERE HERE

Words and Music by
PETER CETERA

Slowly

Sleep-less hours and dream-less nights and far-a-ways.
Same old show in a dif-f'rent town on an-oth-er time.
On the road it's a heav-y load, but I'll get by.

Oo, wish-ing you were here.
(Wish-ing you were here.)

Heav-en knows, and, Lord, it shows when
E-ven though you're far a-way, you're
Pay the price, make a sac-ri-fice and

Copyright © 1974 by BMG Songs, Inc. and Big Elk Music
International Copyright Secured   All Rights Reserved

Dm
Gm7
3fr
C7
Dm
To Coda
I'm a - way.
on my mind.
still I'll try.
Oo,
wish-ing you were here.
(Wish-ing you were here.)
Dm7
E/D
E♭/D
Dm
Oo.
Dm7
E/D
E♭/D
1
Dm
B♭
C
Oo.
2
Dm
B♭
C
And I'd like to change my life,
f

and you know I would, just to be with you tonight, baby, if I could. But I've got my job to do, and I do it well, so I guess that's how it is.

Oo, wishing you were here. Oo, wishing you were

Dm
Dm7
E/D
here.
Oo.
(Wish-ing you _ were here. _)
E♭/D
Dm
B♭
C
D.S. al Coda
(Wish-ing you _ were here. _)
CODA
Dm
C
B♭
C
here.
(Wish-ing you _ were here. _)
Oo,
wish-ing you _ were
Dm7
E/D
E♭/D
Dm
D
Oo.
here.
(Wish-ing you _ were here. _)
8vb

YOU MAKE LOVIN' FUN

Words and Music by
CHRISTINE McVIE

Moderate Rock beat

Sweet, _____ won-der-ful you. _____
don't break the spell.

You make me hap-py with the things you do. _____
It would be dif-f'rent, and you know it will.

Copyright © 1976, 1977 by Fleetwood Mac Music
All Rights Administered by Careers-BMG Music Publishing, Inc.
International Copyright Secured   All Rights Reserved

221

I never did believe in miracles. But I've a feeling it's time to try. I never did believe in the ways of mag - ic.

But I'm be - gin - ning to won - der why.

Don't, You,

you make lov - ing fun.

D.S. al Coda

CODA

Repeat and Fade

THE DECADE SERIES

The Decade Series explores the music of the 1890's to the 1980's through each era's major events and personalities. Each volume features text and photos and over 40 of the decade's top songs, so readers can see how music has acted as a mirror or a catalyst for current events and trends. Each book is arranged for piano, voice & guitar.

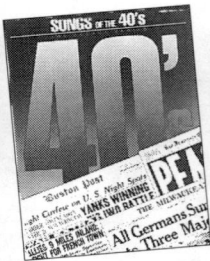

Songs Of The 1890's
Over 50 songs, including: America, The Beautiful • The Band Played On • Hello! Ma Baby • Maple Leaf Rag • My Wild Irish Rose • O Sole Mio • The Sidewalks Of New York • The Stars And Stripes Forever • Ta Ra Ra Boom De Ay • Who Threw The Overalls In Mistress Murphy's Chowder • and more.
_____00311655 ....$12.95

Songs Of The 1900s – 1900-1909
Over 50 favorites, including: Anchors Aweigh • Bill Bailey, Won't You Please Come Home • By The Light Of The Silvery Moon • Fascination • Give My Regards To Broadway • Mary's A Grand Old Name • Meet Me In St. Louis • Shine On Harvest Moon • Sweet Adeline • Take Me Out to the Ball Game • Waltzing Matilda • The Yankee Doodle Boy • You're A Grand Old Flag • and more.
_____00311656 ....$12.95

Songs Of The 1910s
Over 50 classics, including: After You've Gone • Alexander's Ragtime Band • Danny Boy • (Back Home Again) In Indiana • Let Me Call You Sweetheart • My Melancholy Baby • 'Neath The Southern Moon • Oh, You Beautiful Doll • Rock-A-Bye Your Baby With A Dixie Melody • When Irish Eyes Are Smiling • You Made Me Love You • and more.
_____00311657 ....$12.95

Songs Of The 20's
58 songs, featuring: Ain't Misbehavin' • April Showers • Baby Face • California Here I Come • Five Foot Two, Eyes Of Blue • I Can't Give You Anything But Love • Manhattan • Stardust • The Varsity Drag • Who's Sorry Now.
_____00361122 ....$14.95

Songs Of The 30's
61 songs, featuring: All Of Me • The Continental • I Can't Get Started • I'm Getting Sentimental Over You • In The Mood • The Lady Is A Tramp • Love Letters In The Sand • My Funny Valentine • Smoke Gets In Your Eyes • What A Diff'rence A Day Made.
_____00361123 ....$14.95

Songs Of The 40's
61 songs, featuring: Come Rain Or Come Shine • God Bless The Child • How High The Moon • The Last Time I Saw Paris • Moonlight In Vermont • A Nightingale Sang In Berkeley Square • A String Of Pearls • Swinging On A Star • Tuxedo Junction • You'll Never Walk Alone.
_____00361124 ....$14.95

Songs Of The 50's
59 songs, featuring: Blue Suede Shoes • Blue Velvet • Here's That Rainy Day • Love Me Tender • Misty • Rock Around The Clock • Satin Doll • Tammy • Three Coins In The Fountain • Young At Heart.
_____00361125 ....$14.95

Songs Of The 60's
60 songs, featuring: By The Time I Get To Phoenix • California Dreamin' • Can't Help Falling In Love • Downtown • Green Green Grass Of Home • Happy Together • I Want To Hold Your Hand • Love Is Blue • More • Strangers In The Night.
_____00361126 ....$14.95

Songs Of The 70's
More than 45 songs including: Don't Cry For Me Argentina • Feelings • The First Time Ever I Saw Your Face • How Deep Is Your Love • Imagine • Let It Be • Me And Bobby McGee • Piano Man • Reunited • Send In The Clowns • Sometimes When We Touch • Tomorrow • You Don't Bring Me Flowers • You Needed Me.
_____00361127 ....$14.95

Songs Of The 80's
Over 40 of this decade's biggest hits, including: Candle In The Wind • Don't Worry, Be Happy • Ebony And Ivory • Endless Love • Every Breath You Take • Flashdance... What A Feeling • Islands In The Stream • Kokomo • Memory • Sailing • Somewhere Out There • We Built This City • What's Love Got To Do With It • With Or Without You.
_____00490275 ....$14.95

MORE SONGS OF THE DECADE SERIES

Due to popular demand, we are pleased to present these new collections with even more great songs from the 1920s through 1980s. Each book features piano/vocal/guitar arrangements. Perfect for practicing musicians, educators, collectors, and music hobbyists.

More Songs Of The '20s
Over 50 songs, including: Ain't We Got Fun? • All By Myself • Bill • Carolina In The Morning • Fascinating Rhythm • The Hawaiian Wedding Song • I Want To Be Bad • I'm Just Wild About Harry • Malagueña • Nobody Knows You When You're Down And Out • Someone To Watch Over Me • Yes, Sir, That's My Baby • and more.
_____00311647 ....$14.95

More Songs of the '30s
Over 50 songs, including: All The Things You Are • Begin The Beguine • A Fine Romance • I Only Have Eyes For You • In A Sentimental Mood • Just A Gigolo • Let's Call The Whole Thing Off • The Most Beautiful Girl In The World • Mad Dogs And Englishmen • Stompin' At The Savoy • Stormy Weather • Thanks For The Memory • The Very Thought Of You • and more.
_____00311648 ....$14.95

More Songs Of The '40s
Over 60 songs, including: Bali Ha'i • Be Careful, It's My Heart • A Dream Is A Wish Your Heart Makes • Five Guys Named Moe • Is You Is, Or Is You Ain't (Ma' Baby) • The Last Time I Saw Paris • Old Devil Moon • San Antonio Rose • Some Enchanted Evening • Steppin' Out With My Baby • Take The "A" Train • Too Darn Hot • Zip-A-Dee-Doo-Dah • and more.
_____00311649 ....$14.95

More Songs Of The '50s
Over 50 songs, including: All Of You • Blueberry Hill • Chanson D'Amour • Charlie Brown • Do-Re-Mi • Hey, Good Lookin' • Hound Dog • I Could Have Danced All Night • Love And Marriage • Mack The Knife • Mona Lisa • My Favorite Things • Sixteen Tons • (Let Me Be Your) Teddy Bear • That's Amore • Yakety Yak • and more.
_____00311650 ....$14.95

More Songs Of The '60s
Over 60 songs, including: Alfie • Baby Elephant Walk • Bonanza • Born To Be Wild • Eleanor Rigby • The Impossible Dream • Leaving On A Jet Plane • Moon River • Raindrops Keep Fallin' On My Head • Ruby, Don't Take Your Love To Town • Seasons In The Sun • Sweet Caroline • Tell Laura I Love Her • A Time For Us • What The World Needs Now • Wooly Bully • and more.
_____00311651 ....$14.95

More Songs Of The '70s
Over 50 songs, including: Afternoon Delight • All By Myself • American Pie • Billy, Don't Be A Hero • The Candy Man • Happy Days • I Shot The Sheriff • Long Cool Woman (In A Black Dress) • Maggie May • On Broadway • She Believes In Me • She's Always A Woman • Spiders And Snakes • Star Wars • Taxi • You've Got A Friend • and more.
_____00311652 ....$14.95

More Songs Of The '80s
Over 50 songs, including: Addicted To Love • Almost Paradise • Axel F • Call Me • Don't Know Much • Even The Nights Are Better • Footloose • Funkytown • Girls Just Want To Have Fun • The Heat Is On • Karma Chameleon • Longer • Straight Up • Take My Breath Away • Tell Her About It • We're In This Love Together • and more.
_____00311653 ....$14.95

FOR MORE INFORMATION, SEE YOUR LOCAL MUSIC DEALER, OR WRITE TO:

HAL•LEONARD
7777 W. BLUEMOUND RD. P.O. BOX 13819 MILWAUKEE, WI 53213

Prices, availability & contents subject to change without notice.